NEGAHOLICS

NEGAHOLICS

HOW TO RECOVER FROM YOUR ADDICTION TO NEGATIVITY AND TURN YOUR LIFE AROUND

Chérie Carter-Scott

VILLARD BOOKS · NEW YORK · 1989

Library of Congress Cataloging-in-Publication Data

Carter-Scott, Chérie.
Negaholics.

1. Negativism. 2. Self-perception.
3. Self-realization. I. Title.
BF698.35.N44C37 1989   155.2'32   88-37880
ISBN 0-394-57464-8

Designed by Oksana Kushnir

Manufactured in the United States of America
9 8 7 6 5 4 3 2
First edition

DEDICATION

I dedicate this book to all those people who have given
their time, energy, dedication, and love to the
continuation and perpetuation of our Motivation
Management Service, work and the Self Esteem
Workshop.

My two loving and dedicated partners: Lynn Stewart
and Suzanne Eastman, without whom it would not have
been possible.

Lynn is not only my sister, my partner, but she is also
my very dear friend, collaborator, and twin soul. In her
relentless manner, she has been there for me, getting
me through the process of writing this book with fun
and humor. As always she was there when I needed her.

To Warren Bennis, Diane Reverand, and Jim Stein, who
believe in me and coach me in ways I can hear.

To all those who have supported the efforts and
activities of MMS, me, the process, and in particular
this book: Bill Baun, Jacob Blass, Jan Carolan, Peggy
and George Carter, Joann Corona, Peggy Findley, Julie
Inglese, Jerry Kreger, Joan Levinson, Tom Massey,
Goran Milic, Nancy O'Neal, Jerry Preator, Norma
Scriven, Jamie Weinstein, Theo Wells.

To all MMS associates and employees who have given
selflessly and devotedly and have trusted their messages
to align with the work: Mark Abramson, Susan
Abramson, Barbara Adamich, Robert Adamich, Mary
Berley, Barbara Bolton, Bob Bolton, David Bowes, Allen
Bremer, Diane Burney, Christopher Byrnne, John
Carter-Scott, Fred Chase, Pam Cohen, Jim Cohen, Carol
Costello, Sherwood Cummins, Maria Demetriou, Bill
Douglas, Merle Dulien, Mary Lou Einloth, Espie
Ekman, Martha Fateman, Chris Fernandez, Steve Flax,
Valerie Fontaine, Michael Fontaine, Dorine Foster,
James Fox, Ric Giardina, Deborah Gorman, Byron

Gunther, Jill Gurney, George Hain, Kris Hall, Roger
Hannegan, Bob Jukich, Arden Kahlo, David Keller,
Cindy Kelley, Kathy Kirkpatrick, Kathleen Lamb,
Jenny Lang, Russell Levine, Bill Lowe, Anne Marie
Macari, Jan Martin, Kate Martin, Kathi Martin, Rob
Martin, Donna McCarthy, Christine Meacham, Warren
Meacham, Nancy Millar, Bill Millham, Joan Murphy,
Frits Philips, and Christine Philips, Suzy Prudden, Bob
Puckett, Sarah Samuels, Wendy Senna, Sandra Shipley,
Bridget Starri, Kirk Stathes, Ray Stoddard, Judith
Sussman, Alannah Van Boven, Lynne Whiteley-Novy,
Candy Williams, Jan Young, Mary Zick.

To Mary Kelly Untermeyer and Milton Untermeyer,
who did the best they could and gave me the motivation
to search, to find, and to understand.

And in loving memory to Barbra Rasmussen and Jeffrey
Heefner.

I am grateful for my gifts. I am grateful for my friends,
associates, family, and staff who have supported me, and
I am deeply grateful to God for choosing me to bring
this work to myself and others.

All the case studies used in this book were based on
actual sessions with workshop participants, clients of
Motivation Management Service, Inc., or The MMS
Institute. The names have been changed to honor their
confidentiality. It is with gratitude that they are
acknowledged in their anonymity for their contribution
to our work and this book.

CONTENTS

INTRODUCTION

This book is about a condition that is sweeping the nation called negaholism. Negaholism is a syndrome in which people unconsciously limit their own innate abilities, convince themselves that they can't have what they want, and sabotage their wishes, desires, and dreams. This book is about how negaholism manifests itself daily in the lives of normal people. Self-imposed limitations on happiness, joy, and fulfillment contaminate the consciousness of the majority of the population in subtle ways. The beliefs, attitudes, and perceptions which keep us restricted, constrained, and curtailed have reached epidemic proportions. (Data?)

When you read this book, you will recognize either yourself or others who are victims of negaholism. You will also see ways out of the negaholic trap. Using the tools and techniques described in this book will enable you to change old patterns and embark on a whole new way of life. I know, because I was a negaholic, and what I've learned can help you.

In October 1974, I decided to start a business which would help people discover their own answers to perplexing situations in their lives. I knew that I could be a catalyst for individuals to reflect within *meaning what?*

themselves in a safe environment to determine what they truly wanted.

My first client was a friend who had his own business and wanted me to help him sort things out. He was so pleased with the results of our session that he told friends and associates about it. My phone started ringing with requests from people asking whether I would advise them about their careers, their relationships, their living situations, and their future plans.

I told them, quite frankly, that I don't give advice, recommendations, or suggestions. I don't administer a battery of tests. I don't analyze, interpret, or figure out. I will ask provocative questions which will enable you to search within for your answers. You will uncover and discover your own answers to the questions which are puzzling you. The process is similar to prying open an oyster and finding a pearl inside. The treasure—the answer—always resides within, but it is often camouflaged by layers of confusion, doubt, uncertainty, and fear. The challenge is to penetrate through the layers of "I don't know" and pierce through to the "I knows": the pearl within.

As I began "consulting" (which is what I call the questioning process) I found my client's results astonishing. Every person without exception found his true answers within himself. When I say "true" answers, I mean answers that ring inside. Not the "right" answers, which sound good, or the ones you give to be liked or to gain the approval of others, but the ones that feel right in your gut. There was no denying the feeling of rightness. The process was simple and profound.

I was concerned that maybe I needed a special degree, certificate, or license in order to do this work, so I called a friend who was a psychiatrist and asked him if I was doing anything wrong or illegal. He asked if I was psychoanalyzing, prescribing, suggesting, directing, or in any way dispensing advice. I responded that, quite the opposite, I was merely asking open-ended questions, actively listening, and focusing all of my attention on the client; that was all. He said many professionals ask questions, and there was nothing wrong with doing so. Business consultants, retail sales people, even travel agents, ask questions—it enables them to do their jobs better by finding out the information necessary in order to serve the client. He said I didn't need any credentials to ask questions.

An acquaintance, Kathy Kirkpatrick, called me to say that she heard I was doing really good work. I replied that I was merely asking some dumb questions. She claimed that the word on the street was that something different and special seemed to be going on in those sessions and asked if she could sit in. My client agreed to this, and after auditing a session, Kathy commented, "That's amazing! You asked open-ended questions. You suspended judgment. You created a safe environment. You encouraged the client to use his imagination and explore his fantasies. You had no agenda, nor did you know what was coming next, or what was best for him, nor did you give any of your own good ideas."

"I said, "Well, anyone can do that."

"Oh no they can't," she said. "You have a talent!"

"Come *on*," I responded in sheer disbelief, "I just asked some dumb questions."

"I can play music by ear. I can hear a tune, and sit down at the piano and play it," she said. "Can you do that?"

"No, that is truly a gift!" I replied.

"You too have a gift, only most of the world doesn't recognize it as such. You happen to be born with an ability to work with people. Not everyone can do what you have just done. Trust me, I know what I'm saying."

Shortly thereafter, Kathy joined me as a partner in the business. We formulated the organizational workshop, designed to let individuals learn self-management skills. After two years of holding consultations, it became apparent that people who believed in themselves manifested their dreams, while those who didn't sold themselves short. It wasn't enough to help people find out what they wanted. In addition, it was essential to support the belief these people had in themselves, the knowledge that they deserved to have what they wanted and were able to have their dreams come true.

The next challenge was clear: to design a program which

would allow people to unearth, uproot, and expel the part of them that was holding them back and selling out—the part which was keeping them from having what they wanted. The self-esteem workshop was created to help people find the saboteur within, to exorcise the menace of negativity, and to set out on a course of self-love, support, and self-empowerment.

During the past fifteen years, I have conducted workshops in the public sector as well as within corporations. The programs have focused first on the individual and his/her ability to grow and flourish in life. The second focus has helped people with their interpersonal interactions so that they are more effective, both on and off the job. I've consulted in one-to-one sessions as well as in group workshops. The same essential issues were present in my studies and in my work:

- How can I have what I want in my life?
- How can I have the job that utilizes my abilities and skills, gives me a sense of satisfaction, and rewards me monetarily?
- How can I have the intimate relationship that I want?
- How can I have the home environment that I want?
- How can I have the body that I want?
- How can I feel good about myself?
- How can I have my business be the way that I want it?
- How can I design the life that makes me feel as if my dreams have come true?

The process has three parts:

1. determining and/or clarifying what you want,
2. strategizing an action plan,
3. being supported in the realization of the dream.

There is a definite beginning, middle, and end to every problem for which we are consulted. We are not so much interested in the "why" or the "how" as the "what." What do you want? What does it look like? What will it take? What do you need to get there? The process is therapeutic rather than therapy itself. It is not long term, but short term. It is solution-oriented.

The process is so utterly simple that it boggles the mind, because at its very essence is safety, nurture, and encouragement. The process presumes nothing. It reverses the roles of student and teacher, of audience and actor, of spectator and participator. The consultant/facilitator is not an expert but rather a catalyst for discovery, an agent of change, a midwife aiding you in birthing the YOU that you truly want to become.

Abraham Maslow, known as the father of modern motivational theory, based his famous work *Motivation and Personality* on his studies of people as psychological specimens. His theory asserts that individuals are more capable, rational, and self-reliant than previous theories had suggested. The central core of his thesis is that man is an ever-wanting animal. As one want gets satisfied, another surfaces. In his "hierarchy of needs" chart, he showed a five-stage progression—from survival, security, and belongingness, to self-esteem and finally self-actualization.

Having worked with clients throughout the United States, varying in age, sex, race, financial status, and life style, I have found it to be obvious that, although their concerns span a broad spectrum, they follow quite literally the progression outlined in Maslow's chart. There is little similarity between the person who is concerned about basic survival issues such as where he is going to get his next meal, where he will sleep, how he will clothe himself, and the person who is focusing on a career change, a divorce, or life purpose. I have found one consistent, all-pervasive theme that appears to be a major issue to all people regardless of their life condition, status in society, or background.

This fundamental issue has been the source of the majority of my clients' concerns. It is so subtle, so elusive, so evasive that most people don't know what to call it or how to address it. The issue I am referring to has been given many names, including "the voice in my head," "my mind," "the mind chatter," "the gremlin inside," "the monkey on my back," "the critical parent," "my demons," and "the pathological critic."

Have you ever heard these voices? Ask yourself if you have heard a chattering in your head, which in essence was talking to you. See if you can recall a dialogue within your head which was either commenting about you or others. If you have, then you are like the vast majority of adults who inhabit our society.

The concept of negaholism is the result of many years of research, trial and error. All the techniques found in this book have been used by my clients and workshop participants to conquer negaholism.

Conquering negaholism, or overcoming negativity, is what this book is about. It was written to provide you with the tools, tactics, strategies, and ammunition that will allow you, too, to conquer your negaholism and embark upon the road to a happy and joyous life, filled with everything you want.

This book is about discovering the voices in your head, getting them under control, and either abolishing them or having them work for you. The voices tend to operate as if they had a life of their own, and often act as the saboteur.

I have written this book to help you stand up for yourself, claim your rights, tell the truth about what you're feeling and what you want, and learn how:

- to meet the "I can'ts" head on without cringing
- to fortify the "I cans" and build them into a force to be reckoned with
- to have the "I cans" running your life
- to ward off future negattacks
- to maintain a healthy self-image so that negattacks are unlikely or abolished
- to get what you want in your life

The tools and techniques can and will work for you, too, if you will just give them a try.

—Chérie Carter-Scott
Los Angeles, 1988

NEGAHOLICS

ONE

NEGAHOLISM

■

Think for a moment. Do you ever:

- talk yourself out of a relationship because you think the person is out of your league (too attractive, too successful, too rich),
- talk yourself out of a job opportunity because you're afraid that you might not be up to the challenge,
- tell yourself that you can't enter an athletic competition because you've never done it before, or because you don't want to fail,
- talk yourself out of trying something new because you don't want to look stupid (i.e., skiing, windsurfing, horseback riding),
- talk yourself out of buying that fine antique table because you don't trust your taste or you fear that something might happen to it,
- tell yourself that you can't lose the weight that

you want because you don't have the willpower or because you like food too much,

- tell yourself that you needn't bother planning the vacation you want because you know that some crisis will come up at work, demand your attention, and force you to cancel,
- tell yourself you can't have the car you really want because it's too flashy, impractical, or the money would be better spent elsewhere.

If so, read on.

I have devised a quiz. This is not an ordinary quiz. This is the self-assessment tool which will determine to what degree you are a negaholic. In the next five minutes you will know how serious your condition is. By the end of this book you will know yourself better, understand your behavior patterns, and most important, know what to do to change old habits and addictions and see your way clear to recovery.

ARE YOU A NEGAHOLIC?

■

1. Do you sometimes have difficulty getting out of bed in the morning?
2. Do you sometimes focus on all the times you blew it and things didn't work out?
3. Do you often find yourself expecting the worst so as not to be disappointed?
4. Do you sometimes observe yourself feeling anxious when you hear good news in anticipation of the bad that will surely follow?
5. When asked "What do you want?" do you frequently answer "I don't know"?
6. Do you often hear yourself saying "It doesn't matter" when you are asked what you want?

7. Do you often find yourself citing the mistakes, blunders, mishaps, and boo-boos in your past as justification for not taking another risk?
8. When imagining a big goal, do you hear the voices in your head saying "You can't do that . . ." "You'd never be able to . . ."?
9. Do you have difficulty being enthusiastic about your "to-do" list?
10. Do you frequently find fault with little things you do?
11. Do you hear yourself putting yourself down re: what you wear, how you walk, what you say?
12. Do you have lists of things you have never accomplished that you use against yourself?
13. Do you have difficulty celebrating your accomplishments?
14. When you start to imagine your goals, do you hear "Who do you think you are?" in your head?
15. When friends compliment you, do you brush it off, dismiss it, or look for an ulterior motive?
16. When you look in the mirror do you often count the gray hairs and wrinkles?

DO YOU THINK YOU COULD EVER . . .
17. Have the dream home you want?
18. Have the ideal relationship that you want?
19. Make the amount of money that you want?
20. Have the body you want?
21. Have a job that you enjoy, which is satisfying and rewarding?

DO YOU FREQUENTLY GET ANGRY AT YOURSELF . . .
22. For spending too much/or being a cheapskate
23. For eating too much
24. For drinking too much
25. For wasting time?

DO YOU FREQUENTLY FEEL . . .

26. Angry at yourself or others
27. Anxious in general or in specific
28. Confused about what to do
29. Depressed about anything or nothing
30. Hesitant
31. Impatient
32. Insecure
33. Lonely
34. Regretful
35. Unhappy
36. Unloved
37. Worried?

DO YOU SELDOM FEEL . . .

38. Calm
39. Capable
40. Certain
41. Competent
42. Confident
43. Enthusiastic
44. Happy
45. Joyful
46. Lovable
47. Optimistic
48. Powerful
49. Satisfied?
50. Do you constantly work and strive but rarely experience completion and satisfaction?

ARE YOU A NEGAHOLIC?
Scoring Page
In order to determine the degree to which you are addicted to negaholism, score yourself on the negaholic questionnaire:

- give yourself 2 points for every "YES" answer between #1–15
- give yourself 2 points for every "NO" answer between #16–21
- give yourself 2 points for every "YES" answer between #22–50

Now total your score and find yourself on the scale below. If your score is:

0 Congratulate yourself for having a high self-image, high self-esteem, and being well on your way to a healthy, full life.

1–24 A mild case of negaholism. You have very little to worry about. With some affirmations, positive reinforcement, and pats on the back from yourself and loved ones, you will do just fine.

25–40 You have tendencies toward negaholism. It probably runs in your family. If addressed now, you could nip it in the bud. Left unattended, it could grow into something extremely detrimental to your mental health. A consciousness-raising group, a self-esteem workshop, therapy, or self-help groups would be advised. Also read one positive image book per quarter to get yourself on the right track.

41–60 You need to take your condition seriously. Without proper care and attention you will become a certified negaholic. You need some form of positive input each week to turn this condition around. A chart on the wall with stickers and stars, journal writing, listening to audio self-help, positive image tapes in your car or before going to bed, one self-help book per month, and 10 daily written acknowledgments will help cure this advanced condition.

61–80 You are in the danger zone. No longer can you cover up, take things in stride, or hope it will all clear up when you lose the weight, get the job, land the relationship, or move to the right place. Face facts: You are seriously addicted, and you need to come to terms with it. You emotionally beat yourself up mercilessly. There is hope, though—you are not a lost cause. The first step is to acknowledge that you are a negaholic and that you will do what it takes to arrest this addiction.

81–100   You are a confirmed negaholic! You need to declare yourself a negaholic, and take daily measures to arrest this addiction. The addiction has grown to be bigger than you. The negativity is so subtle that you hardly even notice it; it pervades your thoughts and feelings. You need an external program in which to detoxify yourself from the negative demon within. Read this book and take action! Start immediately! A new life is waiting for you now—a positive self-image is in your future.

After scoring the questionnaire, you could be in one of three places. First, you could be ready for the bridge, for the jump that will end it all. Second, you could be worried about your condition, uncertain that there is any hope for you, ready to take on the challenge but fearful that you're the *one* hopeless case . . . Third, you could be excited that someone has written a book about you, and that with a little help from your friends you could cure your negaholism once and for all.

If you are a negaholic, then you wrestle with your interior battlefield every day of your life. The interior battlefield is where a constant war is being waged between two archenemies. These enemies are the two parts of you.

Have you ever been in an audience and watched a speaker, presenter, or entertainer do his routine and secretly thought to yourself, "I could do that. I could do that better than he is doing it. If I had the chance, I would be ten times better. Why, I would be great!"

This is the "I can" side of you. This side wants to toot its own horn and wants a chance to show its stuff. This part believes that you can meet any challenge, and can live your life

exactly as you want to. This part of you is self-sufficient, capable, and self-confident. It is fearless, possesses no self-doubt,
is never confused, and is almost always certain about
everything.

Unfortunately, that's not the whole picture. Life would be
much simpler if you only had to deal with the "I cans." Have
you ever been offered a job that seemed beyond your abilities,
scope, or experience? Did you hear a voice inside saying: "You
can't do that! You've never done anything like that. You'd
better say 'No.' You don't know what you're doing. They're
going to find out that you don't know what you're doing, and
you'll look like a fool."

If you have ever heard voices that sound like this, then
you are familiar with the "I can't" self. This voice is there
primarily to keep you safe, protected from making a fool of
yourself, from being embarrassed or humiliated. This part tells
you "You can't" about almost anything which stretches you
beyond your limits. It is protective and geared toward keeping
you safe. It is full of self-doubt and fear. It is timid and reticent.
I call this part the "I can't" self, because it comes from a fearful,
limited, and doubtful place.

One of the big challenges in life is learning how to manage
the inner battlefield, how to conquer the "I can'ts." Learning
how to develop robust "I cans" and undernourish the "I can'ts"
is a process that takes time.

Negaholism is when the "I can'ts" have taken over and are
running your life. This has happened over a long, slow learning
period, during which you have become addicted to negativity.
As a child you learned early on that you would receive much
more attention for getting hurt, being sick, not cleaning your
plate, leaving your room messy, getting into trouble, telling
lies, and being difficult rather than by behaving well. With
repeated imprinting, you internalized a motivational system
whereby you received attention for the negatives rather than
the positives. Your addiction to negativity is based upon the
physiological, chemical rush you experience every time you
engage in negative thoughts, words, or actions.

DANNY AND THE MORNING BLAHS

■

Danny was a sweet, unassuming, middle-aged man who greeted everyone he saw with a smile and a warm "How are you?" His mousy-brown hair and his slight build gave him the illusion of being almost invisible. His demeanor was apologetic, and he spoke in a nasal tone you had to strain to hear. He seemed a happy sort of person, but you weren't always sure if the smile had been glued on or if it was for real.

One morning in a quiet moment of truth he said to me, "You know it is the strangest thing. Some days I wake up and feel great, and other days I wake up and feel awful. I wake up feeling worried, anxious, and scared about almost everything. There doesn't seem to be any rhyme or reason to it; some days I'm good and some days I'm bad, and I never know until I wake up how I'm going to be. There doesn't seem to be anything that caused the change; just all of a sudden I'm in terrible shape."

I knew what he was talking about. The syndrome is very familiar to me. The work I've done has given me some answers about why it happens and what can be done about it.

I don't want you to think that I'm going to give you a magic potion. I would love to have a convenient abracadabra in my pocket, but it just doesn't work that way in real life. I would love to have an insta-fix which would make everything all better instantly. Unfortunately it takes time, desire, willingness, and commitment to get to the place of self-mastery. This book contains techniques and tools that I will share with you, but the bottom line is that you have to be willing and committed to using and practicing them.

If you were going to be a concert pianist, you wouldn't just practice the day before the concert; you would practice every day of your life in order to prepare yourself for your big moment. By the time the day of the concert arrived you would be ready.

You had already practiced and laid the groundwork. You would feel confident, because you knew what you were doing since you had put in your time practicing. Many people have the desire and even the willingness. The real question is: Are you really committed to having this situation be different in your life?

Many people fear that they can't change. They think that they're creatures of habit: too old, too lazy, or too stuck in their ways. If you are a person who is fearful that you can't change and that you'll always be the way you are, stop worrying. It takes three weeks of repeated behavior to establish a habit, and six weeks of consistent avoidance to break one. It takes time; it doesn't happen overnight, but it does happen. Remember, all things are possible . . . if you have the desire, the willingness, and the commitment.

You need to be patient and persistent, understanding and relentless, compassionate and determined. These are paradoxes in which the challenge is to hold a hard line and to be infinitely gentle with yourself at the same time. This is a new way of relating to yourself. It's not so hard, but it is different. It's all right if you're skeptical; just open up your mental door of possibilities.

This is our journey into the workings of the inner self, the journey that will allow us to start understanding what makes us tick.

WAKING
UP TO
THE WAR
■

I asked Danny to tell me about the last time he awakened feeling bad. He said, "I went to bed the night before, and I was in great shape; the next thing I knew it was morning and I was a wreck."

"When you say you were a wreck, what does that mean?" I asked.

"It was as if I was under an attack. I felt like I was dodging bombs and missiles which were being dropped on my head before I could get out of bed."

"What kind of an attack, Danny?" I probed.

"Anxiety, panic, fear . . . I was being dive-bombed from all angles by a bunch of fighter pilots. I went to bed in a great mood, with a smile on my face, and here I wake up in the middle of World War Three!"

"Tell me what the fighter pilots were saying to you?" I pushed for information.

"They started with the investments I've made which have gone sour, and then they latched onto my relationships with women, and then they started in on my age. Oh! it was just awful," Danny said, shaking his head incessantly.

"Can you tell me the actual words that they were saying?" I urged.

"Yeah, it's not easy to forget. I don't know when it started, because I woke up in the middle of the war. The first voice I remember was saying, 'You really blew it on those investments. Do you know how much money you are going to lose? Everybody else is making money on real estate, and here you are not even breaking even, but losing money! I can't believe you decided to get into such a risky deal: ski machines, of all things! You should have known that the company was undercapitalized and would go bankrupt. You'll never see your money again. How could you blow all your money? Just consider it lost, you'll never get it back. You'll be a pauper, penniless and on the street. Then who will want you? Who wants you anyway? Elaine keeps saying she doesn't want to have sex with you. She keeps giving you those lamebrained excuses. Let's face it: You're a failure, and you're never going to make it! Besides, who would want someone as short as you?' " Danny hung his head and then abruptly raised it and said, "I really felt like I'd been wounded. It was awful!"

After having listened to Danny's wake-up story, I knew his problem. Danny was a negaholic. There was a part of him deep inside that was against him. What's more, the mechanism was out of his control, and, unconsciously, he was addicted to the self-negation pattern. I wanted Danny to understand that the negaholic syndrome is a common affliction, one which affects the majority of our population. There is good news: It is curable.

THE "I CAN/I CAN'T" GAME

■

There are two sides in each one of us: The "I can" self and the "I can't" self are both jockeying for position. Both sides play games to see who gets to be on top. Usually when you are about to enter the stretch zone, go for a big goal, or take a big risk, the "I can't" self comes in and tries to dissuade and distract you. The "I can't" self tries to keep you safe and protected from disappointment and failure. It thinks if you don't risk too much, then you won't be too disappointed, nor will you have quite so far to fall if you fail. This side of you wants to play it safe and hedge your bets. The unfortunate part is that the "I can't" self is a bully, and is usually stronger than the ninety-eight pound "I can" weakling. So it's not too difficult to guess who usually wins these contests.

The problem is that the "I can't" self gets carried away and becomes more than protective; it becomes downright critical. It begins to criticize your wants and to tell you that you can't have them, that they are beyond your grasp, that you're not able to have what you want. If allowed to run wild, the "I can't" self can and will take over the whole show. It will start to dictate who you are, who you aren't, what you can do and what you can have in your life. Since the "I can't" self comes from scarcity and limitations, it is not surprising that it begins to tell you that you can't do or have what you want. It endeavors to keep you within narrow parameters in order to keep you safe and in control.

THE TAKEOVER OF THE "I CAN'TS"

When the "I can'ts" take over and seize hold of you, you are suffering from a "negattack." A negattack is when the "I can'ts" begin to run roughshod all over your dreams and fantasies. Like a band of outlaws, they ravage and plunder with no concern for the tender, fragile, and precious hopes that lurk within. The "I cans" have not organized themselves into a posse to combat the "I can'ts" and head them off at the pass. Far from it, the "I cans" are gentle, loving folk who sit by supportively and get trampled every time the gang rides into town.

WHY IS THE SYNDROME CALLED "NEGAHOLIC"?

Nega = negative, holic = one who is addicted to something. A negaholic is one who is addicted to negativity. *Negare* is a Latin root meaning to deny. The "I can'ts" are denying that the "I cans" are right. Denying means that the "I can'ts" refuse to accept the fact that the "I cans" are capable, competent, able to give you what you want. The "I can'ts" deny that the "I cans" are worthy, lovable, and deserving. A negaholic is one who is victimized by inner forces that are waging a war of self-negation with attitudes, thoughts, words, or behavior. These forces are keeping you trapped in a private dungeon with graffiti all over the walls that say: "You can't be it. You can't do it. You can't have it. So forget it!" The "I can't" self laughs and says "I told you so" when you prove its prophesies right.

NEGAHOLISM TAKES FOUR DIFFERENT FORMS

■

I have separated negaholics into four categories so that you can see how all-pervasive the syndrome is, and how many different forms it takes. Having seen every form of negaholism over the past fifteen years, I have assigned them their appropriate label and grouped them into the categories which suit them. One category really spills over into the next; the negative attitudes and thoughts are usually demonstrated through words and actions.

ATTITUDINAL NEGAHOLICS are successful people who drive themselves relentlessly. To the outsider they appear to have it all together, but inside they are tormented. They are the most subtle form of negaholic because their appearance is crisp, clean, orderly, and aesthetically pleasing. They are usually on top of everything. The negaholics in this group are: The Perfectionist, The Never-Good-Enough Person, and The Slave Driver.

BEHAVIORAL NEGAHOLICS may be succeeding in spite of themselves, but they are most often missing the mark. They try so hard that you don't want to fault them, but their self-sabotage is written all over them. Caught between the discrepancy between their ideas and their actions, they are unable to break out of their behavioral patterns even though they seem to try. This group consists of The Procrastinator, The Pattern Repeater, and The Never-Measure-Up Person. Behavioral negaholics act out the negativity in nonsupportive ways such as too much smoking, overeating, excessive drinking, abuse of drugs, overindulgence in gambling, exercise, TV, work, relationships, sex, and religion.

MENTAL NEGAHOLICS are constantly flogging themselves. They glom on to something they have done or said, lock on to it and won't let go. They are ruthless and indiscriminate, focusing on the past, the present, or the future with criticism, invalidation, judgments, and mental abuse. The Constant Critic, The Comparing Contestant, The Retroactive Fault-Finder, and The Premature Invalidator are all related mental negaholics.

VERBAL NEGAHOLICS are hopeless, helpless, and unable to change. They make negative statements about themselves, others, situations, places, just about anything. Incredibly, they don't have the slightest idea that they are being negative, they think that they are accurately reporting the facts the way they are. In this group are: The Beartrapper, The Constant Complainer, The Herald of Disaster, and, of course, The Gloom and Doomer.

TYPES OF NEGAHOLICS

Successful but Driving Self-Relentlessly	The Perfectionist The Never-Good-Enough Person The Slave Driver	Attitudinal Negaholic
May Be Succeeding But Striving Hard	The Procrastinator The Pattern Repeater The Never-Measure-Up Person	Behavioral Negaholic
Habitually Inflicting Punishment on the Self	The Constant Critics The Comparing Contestant The Retroactive Fault Finder The Premature Invalidator	Mental Negaholic
Hopeless, Helpless, Unable to Change	The Beartrapper The Constant Complainer The Herald of Disasters The Gloom and Doomer	Verbal Negaholic

Sarah's case is instructive. The following three scenarios illustrate the different degrees of negaholism, their manifestation, and her reactions to them.

Sarah is short and muscular, she has an enormous smile that shows her white teeth, and her short brown hair is cropped closely around her face. She teaches exercise classes and is addicted to Diet Coke. Her mood swings are radical; when she is high she will knock you over with her energy, and when she is low she laments and bemoans her fate. She is rarely moderate.

SCENARIO #1:

Sarah feels upset. "I had had a fight with Roger, and that is bothering me. My cat is really sick, I think she might die, and I feel bummed out. I don't know why I am feeling this way. Maybe it has to do with Roger." She just knows she doesn't feel good. She doesn't know why she feels bad. She wants to feel better as fast as she can. She pursues ways to adjust or alter her mood, most probably with Diet Coke.

SCENARIO #2:

Sarah has the same problems as in Scenario #1, but this time she is aware of some chattering in her head, a critical tone accusing her of handling things badly with Roger, and blaming her for her cat's illness. She is aware of the draggy, low-energy feeling she has, and decides to call a friend to brighten her spirits. She picks up the phone.

SCENARIO #3:

Sarah acts out an intense melodrama starring, you guessed it, Sarah as the heroine who is tormented by the screaming meanies in her head. "You blew it with Roger, you were irresponsible with your cat, you never should have gone to bed so late. Why did you yell at your mother? You know it always makes her cry and whimper for days. I can't believe you bought that new outfit, and the stupidity of speeding on that stretch where you know there is a speed trap! Now you have a speeding ticket!

You had to eat that gooey dessert after lunch. And on top of it all, you're broke! God, are you hopeless!"

Sarah has escalated from feeling low to high anxiety. She is bordering on a full-fledged negattack.

Here are three different levels of negaholism. In the first scenario Sarah has a moderate case of negaholism, and a rather limited awareness of her condition. In the second, her condition is actually milder, and the solution is to reach out for support. Reaching out is always an indication that there is a reasonable amount of awareness, and that she is able to acknowledge she could use some help. In the third scenario, Sarah is in chronic condition. She has become self-consumed. The "I can'ts" have taken over and are totally in charge. They are beating her around the head and shoulders with not only how she can't, but how she didn't, and how she shouldn't have, and how she couldn't ever.

THE BROAD RANGE OF ATTITUDINAL NEGAHOLISM

A negaholic attitude can never be satisfied. On a very deep level you believe that it is not possible ever really to enjoy life. A negaholic attitude is any point of view or perception that creates a losing game. Either the standard is set and impossible to live up to, or you can never do enough, be good enough, or have enough to satisfy the relentless dragon which drives you.

There are three types of attitudinal negaholics: The Perfectionist, The Never-Good-Enough Person, and The Slave Driver.

THE PERFECTIONIST
■

The Perfectionist is a cross between good news and bad news. The Perfectionist has high, some might say unreasonable, standards.

An erect, well-dressed business executive with every hair in place, Dwayne's warm, inviting smile and firm handshake as he entered my office conveyed a sense of confidence and control that seemed almost rehearsed.

"I don't know why I'm here, but Robin, my fiancée, said that you were good to talk to about transitions and career changes. I know what I want, and I strategize and plan so that I get what I want."

"What transition or career change are you encountering?" I said, quite interested.

"Well, I'm in the computer business and it's time to make a change. I want to go into the restaurant business," he said in a rather strange way.

"Tell me why you want to get out of computers," I inquired.

"I've had it with computers, and I've learned all I need to know," he said in an imperious tone, his air of self-confidence never wavering. I was confused by what he said. Something didn't jibe between the way he looked and the way he talked. It didn't make sense. I pushed for more information. "What do you mean, you've had it with computers? Tell me what exactly is your present situation?"

"I'm not working right now. You see I have this bad luck of getting stuck working with idiots. They can't do the job right. I try to tell them, even teach them so that they can do it right, but they are so dumb. It's easy for me, so I usually end up doing the job myself." He said this quite proudly.

"Did you quit or were you fired?" I asked with laserlike directness.

"It was a draw. You know, mutual on both sides. My boss

said I wasn't a team player, and I was ready to go, so we just called it quits." He was quite matter of fact about it.

"How many jobs have you had in the last five years?" I asked.

"Four. You see, I learn fast and then get bored. I just like to move on when I've learned all there is for me in a job," he said, avoiding the real issues.

As I questioned Dwayne, it became clear that he wasn't only a loner, but also a perfectionist. He had real difficulties accepting anyone else's shortcomings.

The Perfectionist expects perfection, and anything that falls short of it is unacceptable. He expects it from himself and from everyone around him. The good news is that you will always get outstanding products and services from this person. The bad news is that it is difficult if not impossible to please him, and if you don't measure up, you get the ax. Imperfections are intolerable. The pressure to perform up to his standard is intense. Since there are few people who fill the bill of being perfect, the result is that he feels righteous, better than everyone else, and alone. He comes from "I can do it better myself."

The obvious question is, "How is this person a negaholic?" If you take the psychological oil rig and drill down into the underpinnings of the perfectionistic attitude, there is almost always a deep-seated fear of not being good enough, of being found out, of being inadequate. This is a slightly different twist from "It's never good enough," but at its core it is negaholic.

THE NEVER-GOOD-ENOUGH PERSON

Akin to the Perfectionist's attitude but slightly different is the Never-Good-Enough Person. This type of negaholic constantly and consistently sets standards and goals which are unattainable. These unrealistic expectations create an internal dynamic that reinforces the fact that the person is a loser.

George, a successful restaurateur in his mid-thirties, is never satisfied. A handsome, outgoing, fastidious entrepreneur, his clothes are always in style and his color choices show his artistic bent. He has designed a beautiful environment in an ideal location; people line up outside the door eager to get in, day and night, seven days a week, and yet he is *not* happy. When there is litter on the floor for just a few seconds he is distraught. He will dwell on a tardy employee, an unpressed uniform, an ignored procedure. His point of view is that "It's never good enough!" Working with him is frustrating and demoralizing because he rarely notices what is *right*—the food, customer satisfaction, the service staff, the decor, the location, and the "feeling" in the restaurant. The details that are *wrong* should not eclipse all the great things that need to be noticed and recognized. No matter what George, or anyone around him accomplishes, it is never good enough.

THE
SLAVE
DRIVER
■

The Slave Driver is from the same family as the Never-Good-Enough Person and the Perfectionist negaholic. Slave Driving can be either an attitude or a behavior. It spills over from thought to action. Slave Drivers are usually workaholics as well. They are compelled to work, to work harder, to do one more thing. The Slave Driver has no time to play, only to work, work, work. He sits on your shoulder telling you that you must "write the paper." You think to yourself, "I'd like to go to the movies," and the Slave Driver says "NO! Write the paper." You think, "I'd like to spend some time with my daughter," and the Slave Driver says "NO! Write the paper." You think to yourself,

"I'd like to go shopping," and the Slave Driver says "I told you to write, don't you listen, just go write!"

A wiry, slightly built salesman was obsessed with balancing the books. He would walk at a fast clip, his body bent forward, carrying large accounting pads under his arms. Len was obsessed with the idea that if he didn't do the bookkeeping, the business would go bankrupt. He was so anxious about the bookkeeping that his response was always "I've got to go do the books." If asked any time of the day or night, "Hey, Len, would you like to go out [to the beach, downtown, to the movies, to dinner]," his response was always, "I've gotta go do the books." After a while, it became a joke. "Hey, Len, yeah I know, you've got to go do the books, right?"

NEGAHOLIC BEHAVIORS IN THREE DIMENSIONS
■

Behavioral negaholics trip themselves up time and time again. They appear to be hooked on the behavior and unable to control and stop what they are doing. They are often sweet people you want to help. If you get attracted to negaholics, they possibly might get you to invest more time in their problems than they themselves have invested.

The three types of behavioral negaholics are: The Procrastinator, The Pattern Repeater, and The Never-Measure-Up Person.

THE PROCRASTINATOR
■

Your actions may take the form of procrastination. The *mañana* syndrome seems innocent enough, but it may be the precise behavior which keeps you from meeting deadlines, doing what you say you will do, and reinforcing the fact that you are not up to the challenge.

Paul was in a double-headed situation. A stocky, determined young man with flashing green eyes and a highly volatile personality, he would defend his procrastinations to the end. He was a gofer for a record company.

He would put things off; he also had a tremendous resistance to writing anything down. Since he rarely wrote down his tasks, he would forget and get into trouble with his boss. What he didn't forget, he would put off until later. What Paul didn't understand was that some unforeseen emergency always messes up the best-laid plans.

"You forgot the light bulbs. Did you pick up the mail? Have you gone to the store? When will the shipment be ready? Have you made any of your deliveries?" His boss would grill him. Paul would either feel terrible about himself or he would get defensive about why he didn't get the jobs done. It was not only his boss who asked those questions; Paul also held the same internal dialogue with himself.

He was in a constant state of distress.

"For years I have been saying that I would clean out the garage, and I never seem to get to it. I don't know, at this point it's almost a joke; I just can't get things done." Paul knew he had a problem, but he was stuck. He didn't know how to change his behavior, and he accepted it as part of his personality.

Either Paul was flogging himself or others were chastising him for not doing what he promised he would do. Paul had a difficult time managing himself, but his basic negaholic tendencies were at the root of all of his procrastination.

THE PATTERN REPEATER
■

Self-sabotage may look like repeating old patterns over and over again. It may feel like being stuck in a rut and not knowing how to get out of it. It may look like stringing a psychological fishing line in front of your path, and tripping every time you get really close to your goal.

NINA
AND THE
CANDY BARS
■

Nina and I had a session on her weight. She wasn't obese, just a little plump, nothing serious. She bent forward when she walked, so that the top half of her always arrived before the rest of her. She had a loud voice, and was in constant need of attention. She meant well, but she often promised to do things that never got done.

Nina told me that she wanted to lose fifteen pounds. She said she was willing to do whatever it took. I wasn't certain that I could believe this new commitment, but I wanted to give her the benefit of the doubt. Together we designed an action plan which was workable and would get her what she needed.

I asked her what kind of support she wanted from me and she said, "Remind me when you see me going off track, because I forget. I will probably forget what I told you today, and go against my plan just out of habit."

I agreed. Less then two hours later I was eating a salad at an outdoor café when I saw Nina go strolling by, inhaling a candy bar. I jumped up and darted over to her and asked, "Were you serious when you said you wanted to be reminded?" She was embarrassed, and said sheepishly, "Yes." "Then maybe you want to reconsider your snack," I suggested.

She was grateful for this incident because it jolted her out of an automatic behavior and into examining the truth of her words. She saw that she was saying one thing and doing another. She was sabotaging herself by engaging in behaviors which were the opposite of her wishes. She proceeded to lose twenty pounds in the next six weeks and felt stronger, more self-confident and more capable than ever before.

As Penny, a slightly overweight yet bubbly woman of twenty-eight, put it: "My mind wants my body to be thin, but every time I am around chocolate my hands and mouth act independently; I never know how the chocolate gets to my mouth, but before I know it, it is in my stomach."

Tom, a stocky, fast-paced, high-energy salesman who is a workaholic says the same thing in different words. "I plan to take time off to be with my family, to go on vacation, to putter in the garden, but there is always some emergency with the business which keeps me from getting away. I have the best of intentions, but something always happens which keeps me in the office." The reality of the situation is "counterintention."

Counterintention means that you behave in ways that are in direct opposition to what you said you wanted. It is as if you were playing tennis and you see the ball hitting the right corner baseboard; you hit the ball with a hard, low ground stroke and it goes right into the net, or out of the court, or over to the left, anywhere other than where you intended. This counterintention is the physical manifestation of negaholism, self-sabotage. You are getting the opposite of what you intended. You cannot control your actions in such a way that your intentions and your actions are the same. The really tough part is: You don't know what to do about it.

THE NEVER-MEASURE-UP PERSON

Some people always fall short of the mark. You, no doubt, have heard the expressions "always a bridesmaid, never a bride"; "always in second place." Life is full of reasons, not results; the satisfaction of being, doing, and having exactly what you want is out of reach.

Mark is tall, dark, disheveled, and there is always something slightly wrong with his appearance. He either has a button missing on his shirt, or his socks won't stay up, or his cowlick is out of control. A middle-aged man who drives a gray VW convertible, Mark secretly wishes it were a BMW. He is a bank manager who aspires to be a vice president but never quite makes the grade. He is a good athlete who couldn't run in the 10K because he sprained his ankle two weeks before the race. He is a talented pianist who won't let himself get serious about it because he downplays his ability. He is outgoing, friendly, and gregarious, but inside he firmly believes that he is never going to make it.

MENTAL NEGAHOLISM IN DAILY LIFE
■

Perhaps the most subtle and insidious form of negaholism is mental. Sometimes you will be completely unaware of your own thoughts. You may begin to feel low, withdrawn, or in a funk and have no idea why. Though mental negaholics often transfer their thoughts into negaholic actions, there are mental negaholics who live exclusively in their own private world of self-inflicted punishment. The Constant Critic, The Comparing Contestant, The Retroactive Fault-Finder, and The Premature Invalidator are all different types of mental negaholics.

THE CONSTANT CRITIC
■

Arianna, an art director for an advertising agency, walks down the street minding her own business. She has been with the firm where she works for twenty years, and feels she should be making more money at this stage of her career. She has been examining the alternatives.

She has just come from a job interview, and is uncertain

about how well she did. Her brows are furrowed, and her gait is uneven as she dodges passers-by. She is thinking about the interview: how she acted, what she said, and when she appeared unsure of herself. From out of nowhere she is harangued by a critic. A voice, seemingly from over her shoulder, starts relentlessly criticizing her every move. Everything she said and did in the interview was wrong.

"You said all the wrong things! You sounded so uncertain, and you didn't tell her any of your accomplishments. And the way you sat! Slumped in your chair. You didn't even tell her that you got an award for your artwork in '84. You really blew it," the voice lambastes.

She feels victimized and bad, but without recourse. The constant drone of the critic brings Arianna down lower and lower until she believes that she is worthless, the situation is hopeless, and any action steps are pointless.

There usually is some sort of catalyst for this criticism, like ending a relationship with a loved one or losing a major deal, but often there appears to be no apparent reason for it at all. The criticism may sound like: "You are so fat!," You are so ugly!," "You are so stupid!," "You are so clumsy!" Constant criticism is a more advanced stage of negaholism.

THE COMPARING CONTESTANT

■

Some people need others to bounce off. Comparing yourself to others can be a full-time job, since there are so many contestants.

"Look at her thighs, they're so much thinner than mine." "He has a BMW, and I only have a Honda." "Look at how great their report looks, mine looks so awful." "He has a much better golf game than I could ever have."

Comparing Contestants look at life with a yardstick, comparing themselves to everyone else as if they were involved in a perpetual contest in which they are under constant scrutiny. And guess who never measures up?

For Comparing Contestants, life is a contest and the person who has the most desirable "stuff," the most attractive friends, and the happiest life wins the contest. I'm still not sure who is keeping score, or where the game board is, but I do know that there are a lot of players. The game is about impressing people, having prestige, and making everything seem effortless. Your objective is to impress others with something about you. The game is to look beautiful, to have unlimited wealth, and to be so busy that you need to schedule dinner six months in advance. You go to the latest restaurants, but your critiques are riddled with superlatives: "It was THE best." "It was THE worst."

Brad hated the fact that Earl had a brand-new BMW and he was still driving his old VW. Everytime he saw Earl, he would feel envious. Having a BMW was a symbol of having arrived to Brad. He compared everything. He compared his receding hairline to Hal's, his athletic prowess to Gordon's, and his job status to Fred's. Brad spends most of his time comparing some aspect of himself with someone else. Judging puts Brad in either a superior or an inferior position. He sits in judgment of himself and others constantly.

This game, once started, really has no end, since there is always someone to compare yourself to. You are either better or worse than almost everybody.

THE RETROACTIVE
FAULT-FINDER

Do you find yourself living by clutching and looking into your rearview mirror? You can look into the rearview mirror to see what has just passed and then to dwell on it, blow it out of proportion, and focus on what mistakes were made and how they are irretrievable.

* * *

Clara, from Switzerland, always seemed stuck in a tape loop. She would slide into a refrain of "I should never have left my family. I should have stayed at home and taken care of my mother. I should never have gone to work for that company. I should never have married that man. I should never have cut my long hair." Her rearview mirror reinforced the fact that if she didn't actually do the wrong thing, then whatever she did, she did it wrong.

Retroactive Fault-Finders are steering their lives through rearview mirrors. They are always looking over their shoulders for previous events they can use as ammunition against themselves or others. They use a lot of "shoulds" in their conversations. "I shouldn't have said that," "I should have sent her a birthday card," "I should have called him," "I should have studied harder for the exam," and so on.

Life for this type of negaholic is full of regret, remorse, and self-recrimination. "If only" is a perpetual phrase that torments them with the fact that there was a better way to do it, and they didn't do it that way!

THE
PREMATURE
INVALIDATOR
■

Premature Invalidators can be protective in nature, keeping you from trying new things so you won't be disappointed. On the other hand, they can be poised and ready to pounce on your every mistake.

Have you ever jumped all over yourself *before* you did anything wrong? Sometimes we make real bloopers, which deserve a little ranting and raving. But I'm talking about totally unjustified attacks. Based upon your past performance and negative mindset, you jump to conclusions and indict yourself before you review the facts and the evidence. It's as if you have been convicted before you've ever been tried. It sounds like,

"There you go again. I can't believe that you . . . You always
. . . You never . . ." It could happen almost anywhere or anytime,
but the reality is that this particular negattack is totally unjustified and unfair.

It may happen in the car when you are driving. You may
think that you might have taken the wrong turn, but you are
not sure. Before all the data is in, you wage a full-scale attack
on yourself even though you are just trying to get yourself
where you're going.

Or you've gone out to get the mail and an important call
comes in that you have been waiting for. Your internal voice
launches into a scathing "How could you?" tirade, and there
you are, feeling like an innocent victim pounced upon without
warning. A few minutes later you find out that the person who
called had no time to talk and just wanted to leave some information. You feel chagrined by the brutal way you have
treated yourself. The damage has already been done. You feel
beaten, abused, and scarred.

WHEN
VERBAL
NEGAHOLICS
RUN WILD
■

A verbal negaholic is someone you can't get far enough away
from. Listening to their words can either trigger your own
latent negaholism, or drive you right down the tubes. Focusing
on the negative, highlighting the worst case scenarios, and
obsessing about catastrophies is their full-time job. Unless you
maintain your sense of humor, being around the verbal negaholic can be very depressing. There are four verbal negaholics:
The Beartrapper, The Constant Complainer, The Herald of Disaster, and The Gloom and Doomer.

Jolie was eighteen, and went to Europe with a travel/study
group. It was her first time abroad and she was very excited
about experiencing new cultures, people, foods—in essence,

broadening her horizons. Unfortunately her enthusiasm was not contagious.

Three people on the trip, Esther, Jennie, and Maria, were constantly finding fault with something. Either they wanted hamburgers instead of pâté, or they complained about the toilet paper being too rough, or there was too much walking for their high-heeled shoes. Something was always wrong and they did not hesitate to complain. Their behavior is the direct opposite of being appreciative and gracious. You may be in situations where things aren't right, but the way you go about dealing with the situation is what matters. If you communicate your needs and wants in such a way that people wish to help you get what you want, then a productive outcome can be achieved. If you complain to your friends, who can do nothing about the situation except agree and complain with you, then you are displaying the tendencies of a verbal negaholic.

Verbal negaholics look at life as if it were the proverbial half-empty glass as opposed to the half-full one. The prevailing attitude is that you need to protect yourself, and to expect the worst. "Life is tough," "Wouldn't you know it would happen to me," and "It's just my luck" are famous quotes from verbal negaholics. Their self-fulfilling prophesy is that "life is full of trade-offs," "You need to put up with situations and take what you get because you really can't have what you want." Since these attitudes or beliefs underlie all actions, it is understandable that these negaholics would make themselves right. The way their lives unfold is totally appropriate to their beliefs.

Verbal negaholism is the first cousin of mental negaholism. Verbal negaholics are The Beartrappers, The Constant Complainers, The Heralds of Disaster, and The Gloom and Doomers.

THE BEARTRAPPER
■

The Beartrapper is the person who reaches out for help, support, aid, assistance, or advice, and yet refuses it, explaining that whatever you are proposing won't work, has already been tried, didn't work in the first place, or the situation is more complicated than you can imagine. This is a lose/lose dynamic. Nothing will work. Things are truly hopeless, and the "helper" just doesn't understand. These people are also called "help-rejecting complainers." This syndrome is called "beartrapping" because the person soliciting help opens up a trap into which the helper with the best intentions inserts his foot. The trap is then closed on the foot, and the "bear" or helper feels trapped, annoyed, and angry.

My friend Carol was lamenting to me about her husband. I inadvertently got sucked in. It went like this:

CAROL: Things are really bad.

CHÉRIE: O.K., Maybe it is time to have a talk?

CAROL: Oh, he won't talk! He just ignores me every time I try.

CHÉRIE: Well, maybe you should write him a note, and leave it on his dresser?

CAROL: He throws them in the garbage unopened. He knows I see them and how much it hurts me.

CHÉRIE: Well, why don't you call him at the office?

CAROL: His secretary knows my voice and won't put me through to him.

CHÉRIE: What about sending him a letter registered mail?

CAROL: I've never tried that, but knowing him he'd never be there to receive it.

CHÉRIE: What about telling him straight out that you've set up an appointment with a third party and you want him there?

CAROL: He'd just laugh at me.

CHÉRIE: All right, if you can't talk to him, write him, or call him, then why don't you leave him?

CAROL: Because I don't have any money. He controls all of
          the bank accounts and I have only grocery money.
          How far would that get me?

CHÉRIE: Why don't you file for a divorce?

CAROL: It's money again. Lawyers cost money and I don't
          have any. The house is in his name, as are the bank
          accounts, the charge cards, and all assets.

CHÉRIE: Sounds like you're stuck. I don't know what to tell
          you.

Every suggestion I gave Carol was countered. She was
asking for help, but in reality she was not willing to find a
solution. This does not mean that she was being difficult. Her
problems seem hopeless to her.

THE
CONSTANT
COMPLAINER
■

Take the situation with Neila. She is unaware of her condition,
and people continually shy away from her. She has no idea
why she has no friends. People shy away from her because she
is a negatt. If you come up with a new filing system, she will
say, "It won't work." If you suggest that an employee should
work with a new supervisor, she will say, "She won't do it." If
you encourage her to talk to her boss and discuss her career
goals, she will say, "He won't let me do any of them." After a
while, it becomes apparent that she has a blind spot to anything
positive. It is difficult if not impossible for her to hear her own
attitudes. She doesn't know that she is being negative. Her
attitudes and beliefs are imbedded so deeply within her reality
structure that she looks at life through this negaholic filter
system. She is unaware that a system exists, and believes that
"life's just like that!"

THE HERALD
OF DISASTER
■

"Oh NO, we're going to have an earthquake and we're all going to die!" "I won't be able to pay the rent, I'll be evicted, and end up a bag lady on the street, homeless." Did that thought ever cross your mind? Research shows that one of the biggest fears which people secretly harbor is the fear of being one of the homeless.

Try this on for size: "I know he's going to leave. Just like all the rest. I'll be abandoned and alone. That's my lot in life; I'm just meant to be old and alone, that's my plight."

You are a walking disaster film. You don't expect the worst, you anticipate disasters, tragedies, and calamities. Fear is your middle name, and you live in a state of imagining the worst that can happen.

Mary Alice, a dutiful housewife from the Midwest, a committeewoman who devotes her time to charities, is busy warning about the impending disasters. She is wiry and petite, a pageboy haircut framing her sharp features. She is intense and dogmatic in her proclamations. Last spring, Mary Alice called all her friends in California to warn them that on account of prophesies in the Bible they should pack up all their things and move to the Midwest.

"California is going to fall into the ocean," she said. "From Santa Barbara to San Diego, the entire coastline is going to fall into the sea. You must move before the summer of 1990, or it'll be a disaster," Mary Alice announced in a high-pitched hysterical tone.

Mary Alice is also convinced that the Midwest will dry up from the drought, resulting in crop failure and famine throughout the country.

The latest calamity is that we are all going to die of terminal diseases. She is predicting another stockmarket crash within the next three years, and if disease and financial ruin don't get us, then we will all get wiped out by a nuclear attack. Mary Alice wants everyone to be prepared for disasters, and she takes her job as a Herald quite seriously.

THE GLOOM
AND
DOOMER
■

A first cousin of the Herald of Disaster is the Gloom and Doomer. The difference between the two is that Heralds of Disaster are more panicky and focus on specific events. Their tone is different, urgent, frantic, and borderline hysterical. All their statements end in exclamation points. The Gloom and Doomers have a hopeless tone to them. They are more resigned to things not working out and they don't get excited or upset about anything. In fact their reactions are dead. "It can't be done, if it hasn't been done before it isn't going to be done now, and you aren't going to do any different, so don't even try." These are the people who continuously told the Wright brothers to give up, to forget it, who said, "If man were meant to fly, God would have given him wings." If you have a new invention, don't tell one of them, because they will only throw dirt on your sparks.

Ernie was trying to plan a last-minute promotion for his advertising company. After a stimulating brainstorming session, he thought of the perfect gift to launch the program.

"The aqua T-shirt with the white company logo printed on the front is the perfect way to end the program!" Ernie said triumphantly. "It's too bad that we couldn't pull it off. There is no way we could get those produced in one day. It's just too bad that we didn't think of this sooner."

Right on the heels of his great idea were all the reasons why it couldn't possibly happen. Ernie believed that either they wouldn't have the quantity needed in stock, or the T-shirt colors wouldn't be right, or they couldn't imprint them in the limited time frame. He almost gave up on the idea before he tried to see if it was possible. It wasn't until his secretary grabbed the idea and ran with it and actually produced the T-shirts in less than six hours, that Ernie started to be a believer. The T-shirts happened in a day, but Ernie's attitude didn't change in a day. But this *was* the beginning of Ernie believing in the impossible.

SELF-SABOTAGE, OR SHOOTING YOURSELF IN THE FOOT
∎

All four forms of negaholism—mental, attitudinal, verbal, and behavioral—are various ways in which we sabotage the self. Self-sabotage is the conscious or unconscious thoughts or actions that get in your way so you can't have what you want. Whenever a person engages in an activity which is self-sabotaging or self-deprecating, he is displaying negaholic behavior.

Shirley, an underwriter for an insurance company, aspires to become an officer in the company. She has a bad habit which works against her: she gossips, talks about people behind their backs in negative ways, and almost always gets caught up in the machinery of the rumor mill. She has made so many enemies in the company that people don't want to work for her or even be around her. People don't trust her, or want to disclose any information about themselves which could be used against them. People continuously say that she is shooting herself in the foot.

"I don't understand why, after being in the company for ten years and doing a better job than anyone in the department, they don't think of me for a promotion," Shirley says incredulously. She simply doesn't understand what she is doing wrong, but she does it over and over again.

Very often the unconscious saboteur lies waiting for just the right moment to undermine your intentions. Oversleeping before a final exam, forgetting to pay your phone bill and having your phone turned off, running out of gas before an appointment, remembering a phone call a day too late, leaving important papers on the plane, staying out late the night before an important meeting and waking up tired or hungover—all these are subtle, simple, and insidious ways in which you sabotage yourself regularly.

This behavior is usually deeply rooted, but it is, in fact, curable. This condition is so widespread that there are hardly any people raised in our society who do not engage in some form of self-sabotage. If you are a negaholic, consider yourself normal. That's the good news. But you might want to go beyond normal. You might want to pursue being exceptional, memorable, and noteworthy rather than normal and average. This is your opportunity to go beyond your programmed negaholism.

If you are ready to go beyond normal and average, then read on. You're probably curious as to how you got this way.

TWO

HOW
IT ALL
HAPPENED

■

WHAT
DID
YOU DO TO
DESERVE THIS?
■

How did a nice person like you get into a place like
this? After all, you're a nice person, you do your job,
you hold the door for old people, you're kind to animals, and you try not to hurt anyone. You pay your
taxes, you register to vote, you call your mother
every Sunday, and you don't litter the streets. You're
considerate, responsible, and polite.

So, you ask yourself, "How did this happen to
me? How did I get this way? What did I do to deserve
to have this condition?"

The way you are today is a direct result of how
you were parented, educated, and raised. The beliefs

you have about your capability, relate back to early childhood experiences, when you made decisions about yourself and then formulated beliefs which have governed your entire life.

The voices in your head may say: "I had a wonderful childhood. My parents gave us kids everything. They were great. We really loved one another, and we had such good times." All these comments may seem true to you, and in fact they very well may be, but there is a relationship between what happened then and how you are now.

It is normal to defend your parents, to argue that they did the best they could, to explain their situation, their pressures, and their limitations. And what's more, it's probably all true. The hardest part of examining the origin of your negaholism is coming to terms with the fact that "they," your parents, had a key role in the negaholism which you inherited and developed.

Your parents may have been the model parents to whom you compared yourself and never measured up. You may feel as if you always fall short of the mark they made in your eyes, on the community, or on the world. Perhaps they may have only wanted the best for you, and set high standards in hopes that you would live up to your potential. As a result, you may have turned out to be your own worst critic, driving yourself relentlessly to produce and perform in order to gain the approval that you always wanted.

Your parents might have been warm and loving toward you, and you somehow developed guilt feelings for having such great parents when your friends seemed to be raised in difficult situations. Maybe your parents, with the best of intentions, passed on to you their own limiting beliefs, ones that may have been true in their day, but may be false today. What if they were stressed at times and took their frustrations out on you? You, in turn, may have internalized their outbursts as your fault and blamed yourself for their actions.

Perhaps one or both of your primary caretakers were ill, or one may have been an alcoholic. You may have felt responsible for any or all of this.

It doesn't seem to matter whether your parents were wonderful, average, or dreadful. The end result is the same. If you are a negaholic, you formed a set of self-protective decisions and beliefs which reinforced the fact that "You couldn't, you shouldn't, and mustn't *something*." Hence the seedlings of negaholism. In silent, subtle moments of internal decision-making you chose not to trust your own inner sense of rightness.

I have worked with individuals who have come from extremely abusive homes and with those who were raised in apple-pie "happy" homes: Negaholism is ever-present. Only the degree to which a person is driven by the "I can'ts" varies.

But where do the "I can'ts" come from? How do they become imprinted? When do we take them on as our own? Why do we do it? These are good questions and deserve a thoughtful response, but first it is essential that the issue of loyalty be addressed.

LOYALTY
ABOVE
ALL ELSE
■

Your parents brought you into the world. They gave you life, and nourished you so that you grew into who you are today. They are key people in the formation of your identity, your self-concept, and your orientation to the world. You have them to thank and, in truth, to blame for how you turned out. They probably did the best they could, given the information and the tools which were available to them. Unfortunately, parenting is a role for which we are ill-prepared and untrained. For the most part, your parents reared you in much the same way that they themselves were parented. The legacy gets passed down from generation to generation. Right or wrong, we hand down our psychological "parents" in much the same way as we pass on family photographs, linens, and china. With photographs, you can make your own observations and draw your own conclusions. With psychological baggage, you usually inherit or construct a skewed picture of reality.

It may sound something like this: "My parents were so wonderful. They scrimped and saved and went without so that we could have an education and a roof over our heads. My mother lived for us, and did everything for us." Now this may be true, but there may be ways in which it backfired. Perhaps you took on the guilt for their "going without" in order to provide for you. Perhaps you drive yourself relentlessly in order to justify all the sacrifices which they endured. Perhaps you saw the self-sacrifice and suffering which they experienced, and felt as if you were the cause of their pain and hardship. Whatever the outcome, it is rare that you would end up without a trace of negaholism.

Part of being a child is the inheritance of a set of assumptions which underlie all our perceptions about our families. The characteristics I am referring to appear to be so natural that we don't even perceive them as tendencies. The basic assumptions which block your ability to discern the origin of your negaholism are:

AN UNCONSCIOUS LOYALTY TOWARD YOUR PARENTS

No matter how well or how poorly you were treated by your family, how blissful or traumatic your experience of childhood was, your innate loyalty toward your family overrides everything.

Karen came in for a consulting session to find out which career she wanted to pursue. As we probed her likes and dislikes, her wants and dreams, she drew much of her information from childhood experiences, which is quite normal. During the conversation, clues began to leak out which were contrary to the ideal family picture she had previously recounted. The reality was antithetical to her rose-colored view. In fact, both her parents had been alcoholics; she was physically and mentally abused by her mother and her sister; and no real, honest communication ever took place in her home.

SELECTED
AMNESIA
REGARDING
PAST INCIDENTS
■

As a result of your loyalty toward your family, you may have blocked hurt feelings, painful incidents, and/or traumatic memories from the past. Your survival mechanism probably has skillfully edited out those experiences which flawed your perfect picture and made it impossible to be integrated into your happy family fantasy scenario.

To talk with Karen, you would never suspect that anything was awry, since she had constructed her life story from her heart's desires and not from the reality of the situation. Karen was not lying; she had unconsciously and selectively stored in her mind only those incidents which were happy memories.

Karen's coping mechanisms ceased when she stopped smoking, an activity which served as the glue holding the pieces of the picture together. It was very difficult for Karen to come to terms with the fact that her unconscious loyalty toward her family had overridden the reality of the situation.

Her mother was extremely proud of the fact that people could come to visit any time, day or night, and never know that she had five children. The children were always out of sight, engaged in some quiet, neat activity, and the house was in apple-pie order. Her mother placed a high priority on order and quiet. She didn't anticipate that such a highly controlled and ordered environment could affect the development of the children. As it turned out, of the five siblings in Karen's family, one committed suicide, one is in a mental institution, one refused ever to leave home, and one is an alcoholic. Karen herself married an alcoholic, subsequently got divorced, and is struggling to cope with life as best she can. None of the siblings have children of their own, and probably never will.

ROSE-COLORED GLASSES ARE USED IN HINDSIGHT
■

Psychologically speaking, you put on rose-colored glasses in order to see the past in the best possible light. Incidents are recalled that give your parents the benefit of the doubt, at times skewing the facts, justifying and explaining your parents' behavior so that the past fits within the fantasy scenario which you have skillfully constructed.

On the exterior, Karen, a thirty-seven-year-old woman, is happy, motivated, cheerful, fun-loving, competent, open, and a thoroughly delightful person to have around. To talk to her, you would think that she had a perfect childhood. She would describe her parents and four siblings as loving, happy, and wonderful people. She had great memories of summer vacations and fishing trips during childhood. She loved her family and wanted them all to be happy. Karen had painted a rosy picture of her life not because she was fabricating the past, but rather because she made the best of everything in order to survive, and found a way to keep her spirit alive by being cheerful and happy no matter what. When sad feelings would surface, specifically around the issue of relationships, Karen would put on her happy face and forge ahead.

YOUR TRUE
FEELINGS WERE
OFTEN DENIED
OR SUPPRESSED

In order for you to survive, function, and integrate into your family and society, it was necessary for you to deny, suppress, and sublimate those feelings which were deemed unacceptable. Many feelings were probably declared unacceptable, and, appropriately, you sought euphemistic ways of dealing with them. They were either avoided altogether, denied, or completely suppressed.

At the urging of her doctor, Karen finally stopped smoking. When she did, she realized how difficult it was. She discovered underneath the deep inhalations some old unresolved feelings which she obscured by smoking. Without the smoking mechanism to anesthetize the feelings, she started to feel anxious, nervous, and on edge. She would wake up in the morning feeling anxious and resist getting out of bed. She didn't know what was going on, and was fearful that something was wrong with her. She started feeling irritable and cranky. She began to feel disoriented and had difficulty figuring out what she liked or wanted. She went out with friends who would ask her offhandedly, "What do you want to do?" or "What do you want to eat?" Her response more often than not was "I don't know. What do *you* want?" Out of touch with her feelings and her wants, she would defer to others. She sought to be accommodating and acquiescent, and became resentful later when she didn't have a good time.

After several sessions, Karen began to listen to her own words, to own the painful reality which she had previously denied, and to come to terms with the truth she had been unwilling to deal with. Her commitment to having a healthy and happy life enabled her to face the truth, own the past, and embark on the road to recovery.

These basic assumptions helped Karen survive childhood

and adolescence. Karen is not alone in this. Almost all of us have inherited these same assumptions about those who raised us. What complicates matters is that this veil of assumptions is not flawless, but moth-eaten and filled with holes. These holes allow pieces of reality—undesirable facts from the past which confuse the rose-colored picture—to pass through the scrim.

We all find ways to put on rose-colored glasses and make the unpleasant realities of life go away. It is one of our ways of coping with painful realities we can't handle. Our coping mechanisms are different, but the end result is the same.

I understood Karen's situation, and I felt I could relate to the denial.

I grew up in the fifties and sixties, when television was considered the hottest new gadget, a technological break-through as well as exciting family entertainment. I spent countless hours watching "perfect families" relate to one another in ideal ways. I dreamed of being Betty in *Father Knows Best*, or having Donna Reed for my mother. I fantasized about marrying one of *My Three Sons*, or even meeting Ricky Nelson from *Ozzie and Harriet*. I never missed *Make Room for Daddy* or an episode of *Leave it to Beaver*. In fact, *My Little Margie*, and *Oh, Susanna* were my role models. My home wasn't fun, and I was looking for the perfect family to identify with. By watching these perfect families on TV, I believed that they existed, I wanted to be a part of all the fun, and I projected myself into a world of make-believe which was much more appealing than reality.

I noticed that my parents wanted the neighbors to think our family was just like that of *Ozzie and Harriet*. The whole family went to church every Sunday. In public we were the perfect children, polite, sweet, and well behaved. Everyone played his part. Everyone believed that we were the perfect family, just like those families on TV. The only difference was that Mommy was an alcoholic. If we were the perfect family and were so happy, why was she drunk every day? We did not address these questions; we ignored the obvious. We put on the

rose-colored glasses and acted as if the imperfections didn't
exist. It was our unspoken contract: We don't discuss Mommy's
condition. This loyalty to the family system of ignoring the
painful reality which stared us in the face every day of our
lives was so pervasive that it overrode all other instincts and
inclinations. After all, they were our parents and they made
the rules.

If your loyalty toward your family has not affected you in
any of these ways, and if you are able to look the past squarely
in the face with no denial and tell the truth without superlatives, congratulations: You are the exception, and not the rule.
You are now ready to pursue the origin of negaholism.

THE
ORIGIN
OF NEGAHOLISM
■

The origin of negaholism is much like that of the chicken and
the egg. It never starts or ends, but is passed on from generation
to generation. It is a legacy of unconsciousness and denial
which is rarely ever examined but handed down from parents
to children to grandchildren like an inheritance.

THE
HISTORY
OF NEGAHOLICS
■

Long ago, in the time of cave dwellers, life was simpler: It was
about survival. Food, shelter, and water were the main focuses.
Staying alive was paramount. Dealing with the elements, the
animals, and the hazards of daily living was all-consuming.

As civilizations developed, people evolved from solitary
cave dwellers to clans, to family dynasties. Man became more
sophisticated and established social mores and structures. The
marriage institution evolved as the socially acceptable and le-

gal way of handling coupling. Prearranged marriages were commonplace among wealthy families in order to ensure that bloodlines were kept pure. The primary motivations for marrying were propagating homogenous groups: racial, ethnic, and religious. Elitism, maintaining control of power, and merging for political purposes governed the mating ritual.

I'm not saying that the only reasons people coupled were economic necessity, political motivation, or social acceptability. It is important to examine history in order to see how you got to be where you are. History has dictated the tradition to which you fall prey.

Following our time track up to the present: The need for political, religious, and social freedom motivated the European pioneers to search out and find the New World. Roles were clearly defined for those who came there. Coupling, as in Europe, was still an economic necessity, as well as the socially acceptable thing to do. The man provided food, shelter, and protection for the family, and the woman provided the homemaking, child raising, and nurturing. On a physical level, this rate of exchange worked as an interdependent system. She provided her skills and abilities, he provided his. There was sufficient reason for coupling: to create a complete synergistic unit in which everyone's needs would be met.

The underlying belief, at least for our ancestors, was that each person is incomplete by himself. This may have been the case with your parents, but somewhere in the folds between the generations an emotional as well as a physical and economic need for coupling emerged.

On an emotional level, coupling with another person made each person whole, complete, and provided companionship. Each person looked to the other to be his/her other half, to fill up the deficiencies and make him O.K. in his own eyes as well as in the eyes of others. The giving/getting relationship was Yankelovich motivated by "needing" the other person, much the same way the economic relationship was motivated.

Women experienced pressure to get married so that they would be taken care of and protected. Economic dependence was critical to women, who had no means of supporting themselves and were totally dependent upon men. Women automatically compared themselves with one another because there was, in fact, real competition. They were competing for the men, the breadwinners. Men, on the other hand, competed with one another for the most desirable woman. If a woman could attract the cream of the crop, so to speak, it meant that she was desirable.

If you could put on your grandparents' mind-set and quietly listen to their inner dialogue, it might sound like this:

"If I can get you to love me, then I can't be all bad. At least *someone* wants me. Maybe I am lovable after all!" This thought reinforces the "I cans," which bolsters the person's feeling of desirability.

On the other hand, your grandparents' "I can'ts" are vying for center stage, saying:

"I've been successful in conning this person into thinking that I'm something I'm not. I really pulled the wool over his/her eyes. What kind of a jerk is s/he anyway that s/he would choose *me* to be with. There's got to be something wrong with this person. What did I see in him/her in the first place?"

Frequently there are underlying and unconscious motives which drive the motivation for coupling beyond love, companionship, and simple economics.

In examining how people end up together, and why they choose each other, let's return to Karen's situation.

THE
ROOTS
OF THE TREE
■

During our session, Karen described her grandparents:

"My grandmother was Dutch and her thinking was from the old country. She died before my mother was twelve, and my father was an orphan with limited experience of parenting. When my grandfather died of a heart attack, she was alone in the world. She looked at my dad as her last chance to get married, have children, and be taken care of.

"Under the guise of discipline, my mother was abused both physically and mentally as a young girl. It stands to reason that she probably thought such abuse was normal. I think she thought that beating us kids was the way to make us better people. Whether Mom liked the way her mother treated her or not, she believed that this was just part of her job. She associated abuse with parental responsibility. Come to think of it, she probably never thought about it at all, but just did what was done to her. Mom's childhood home was chaotic and disorganized, so she believed that maintaining a clean, neat, and quiet home was providing a stable environment which would be the best possible world for her children.

"Dad believed that if he could at least maintain peace in the home, then he could hold the family together. If he could hold the family together, then the children wouldn't have to go to an orphanage, which would mean that he was a success as a father. Both my parents thought that they were doing a good job, since they were improving on their own childhood circumstances. And in fact they were," Karen said honestly.

DON'T LEAVE ME!

■

Karen's parents stayed together for any one of the following reasons:

- to have their emotional needs met for the first time
- to feel whole, complete, and sufficient
- to feel valid, deserving, and worthy of being loved
- to prove to the world that they are lovable (to someone)
- to avoid being alone
- to avoid abandonment

WHAT
ABOUT
ME?
■

Perhaps your parents, like Karen's, had to come to terms with
the reality that they probably never would get their emotional
needs met. At the same time their mate was expected to meet
their unfulfilled emotional needs. This compounded the anxiety
and pressure to be adequate, and perform up to standard. The
double bind your parents faced was the inability for each to
get what they needed while simultaneously being expected to
fulfill the emotional needs of their partner. Both your parents
continued the legacy which had been handed down to them.

THE
HONEYMOON
IS OVER
■

There was a point in time when your parents might have felt
that the honeymoon was over. Their perceptions began to
change. Mannerisms, behaviors, and attitudes which once were
appealing became a source of annoyance and turned into ag-
gravations. The picking started and continued.

"If she could lose just a few pounds. That laugh is so shrill.
Those socks are too short, and I can't stand the way he drives.
He watches too much TV. She is so uptight about money," your
parents might have secretly thought.

TURNING
PRINCES
INTO FROGS
■

Negaholics are champions at turning a would-be prince or princess into a frog. If one of your parents believed deep down that

he deserved to be with a frog, then even if his princess demonstrated love for him, he would have transformed her into a
frog. If his self-concept could not allow a princess to really love
him, then he would constantly be searching for the frog within.
He would have had his magnifying glass raised in search of
the tragic flaw. If it were not readily apparent, then he would
have caused one to appear in order to make himself right.

"Ah-ha! There it is, I knew it all the time. Why would I
want to be with someone who would choose me as a mate?"
After all, if his self-fulfilling prophesy was "I only end up with
frogs anyway," then he would make his prophesy come true
regardless of whether his princess was a genuine frog or merely
in disguise.

IN
SEARCH OF
THE TRAGIC
FLAW
■

If anyone searches hard enough, he is likely to uncover the
other person's "I can'ts." If you unearth enough "I can'ts," then
the result is a full-blown frog!

Picture your parents both searching for each other's flaws.
The game is to camouflage their own "I can'ts" and expose their
mate's "I can'ts." The more "I can'ts" that emerge, the greater
the need to expose their partner's "I can'ts" to balance out their
own. This is a vicious cycle that can never be won.

If his mate has no "I can'ts," he makes her look bad by
comparison, but on the other hand, if she is loaded with "I
can'ts" then he's stuck with a loser, a giant frog.

DO
YOU REALLY
LOVE ME?
PROVE IT
■

Your parents then spent an inordinate amount of time testing the relationship, to determine whether their mate was a prince or princess, a frog, a moron, or whether she or he really did love him or her. They may have done everything in their power to drive their spouse away, to cause their partner to remove his or her love in order to prove that she or he was unlovable.

Many secret insecurities and hidden inadequacies may have come to the surface in an attempt to chase away what they had looked for their entire life.

If you get to be right about the fact that "nobody loves you, and nobody will ever love you" you have successfully confirmed your secret suspicions, validated your negative internal voice, and reinforced your negaholism. This is justifiable misery!

Still focusing on your parents: While part of him is driving her away the other part is drawing her closer, desperate to have her love him. The "I can" part has a foot on the accelerator pedal of life, saying "I can have what I want. I can have the relationship I've always wanted. I can be happy with one person. It is possible that I have found my soul mate. I deserve to be happy with the person of my dreams."

While the "I can" part is hoping that fairy tales do come true, the "I can't" part has a foot on the brake pedal of life, saying, "There's got to be something wrong with this person. What is her problem? On the surface she is fine, but underneath there must be a tragic flaw. This is too good to be true. Don't get your hopes up, you'll only be disappointed. She'll end up being like all the rest. You're only dreaming. You *can't* really have what you want."

Still another part of your parents is in "high idle," hoping "If I can get this person to love me, then I can't be all bad. At least *someone* wants me. Maybe I'm lovable after all! This'll show them [parents, teachers, past lovers, and past spouses] that I am lovable, that I didn't ruin our [past] relationship. And maybe, just maybe, I won't have to be abandoned again!"

CO-CREATION: THE CURE-ALL

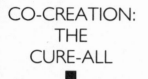

Unable to meet their own needs and incapable of meeting each other's, the couple, your parents, look outside themselves to a third possible alternative. What about a baby! A baby would give them a joint focus, something to create together, a way to partner that is as natural as life itself. The way out of the power struggle is to have a baby. The new hope, the new ray of light, is seen as having a child together. This will address the unmet emotional needs and satisfy both partners by focusing on a third and innocent party to make everything all right. Or so they hope.

WELCOME TO YOUR DYSFUNCTIONAL HOME

A child is born (you) to two people who are disillusioned about their prince/princess and their real-life fairy tale that hasn't turned out the way it did in the books. You may protest, now, on account of your unconscious loyalty toward your parents, but hang in there. Your parents are looking to you, the child, to meet their emotional needs; and you, the child, newborn and helpless, have *only* needs. Since you, the child, cannot get your needs met by your parents, you feel to blame for not getting what you need.

As a tiny infant, you cannot differentiate between yourself and your environment. You haven't any boundaries, and so you

are a part of everything that happens to you. And this is where
it all starts.

YOU
DID IT,
YOU ARE
TO BLAME!
■

You feel everything, and since you are completely "self-
centered" you experience being both the cause and the effect
of all that goes on around you. You, the child, unknowingly
will take the blame for everything that you feel transpiring in
the relationship between your two parents. In the dysfunctional
family, the child will take on all the problems; they are all his
fault. When you are imprinted with the experience of feeling
flawed because your parents could not meet your needs, as well
as the belief that you are the cause of the discord within their
relationship, you then become a negaholic. Since you are loyal
toward your parents and family, you have internalized the
shame and idolized your family.

John Bradshaw in *The Family* quotes Gershen Kaufman,
who in his book *Shame* defines shame: "Shame differs greatly
from the feeling of guilt. Guilt says I've *done* something wrong;
shame says there *is* something wrong with me. Guilt says I've
made a mistake; shame says I *am* a mistake. Guilt says what
I *did* was not good; shame says I *am* no good."

THE
LAYERS
OF THE
ONION SKIN
■

As a developing negaholic, the child believes that he is essen-
tially bad. At your core you are able and worthy, hence the "I
cans." On top of the "I cans" is the next layer: the belief that

you are unworthy, unlovable, unable, insufficient, and inadequate, based upon the imprinting by family and/or society. These are the roots of the "I can'ts." Since these feelings are denied, avoided, discounted, and suppressed, you can't come to terms with your innermost feelings. Instead you must adapt a persona or false self in order to cope with the world. This is a second layer of "I can," or a coping mechanism which is a façade. The compulsive drive to feel whole, complete, adequate, and euphoric in any form comes from the innate emptiness or void inside. Your pursuit of inner peace or wholeness takes any form in order to:

- numb the pain, to cease the torment temporarily
- feel good, get high, experience pleasure, and/or euphoria
- validate your parents, demonstrate your loyalty
- once again abandon yourself, in much the same way as your family abandoned you

THE PERPETUATION
OF THE
SELF-TORMENTING CYCLE
■

The self-tormenting cycle looks like the chart on the following page.

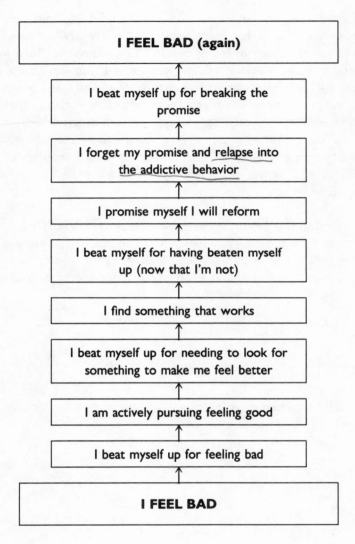

THE
PUZZLE
OF PARENTING
■

Parenting is one of the most important roles a person can fulfill as an adult in our society. For the most part, we parent the way we were parented. "They did the best they could, and it seemed to work out O.K., so I'll do it the same way" is one approach. Or, conversely, we think: "They did it all wrong, and I'm going to do the exact opposite, because they really screwed me up!" Either way you are acting out of a reaction mode, and not from a place of choice.

A PLACE OF CHOICE

Babette, a tall strawberry-blonde restaurateur who was in partnership with her husband, came to talk to me about her teenage daughter. Both parents were being driven crazy by her lack of cooperation within the family. "She stays out all night, her room's a mess, she is never here for meals. She doesn't want to talk to either one of us. I'm fed up and I want to throw her out, but I feel so guilty for feeling this way. I feel powerless and helpless around my own child. I hear words coming out of my mouth that sound just like my mother, and I swore I'd never be like my mother."

I asked Babette how she would want the relationship to be with her daughter. We looked at a series of alternatives: yelling and screaming just like her mother did; sitting down and talking it through calmly at a time other than in the middle of the fury; calling in a family friend whom Wendy, the daughter, respected; or having a session with me as a neutral fair witness. Babette was caught between being exactly like her mother, and not knowing any other way to behave as a parent. She had no choice but to be just like her mother.

DEF FOR LIES.

L.E.S.

THE
POWER
OF CHOICE

■

Choice is a process whereby you examine all the alternatives, and select freely what you want. Choice is informed, aware, and conscious. It is educated and deliberate. When you operate from choice, you have examined the alternatives, the ramifications, and the consequences. Choice is an integrative approach—you put your whole self into the process. You have exercised discretion, integrated your intellect, your intuition, and your feelings, and arrived at a course of action which feels peaceful and "right" inside.

SORRY,
NO DRESS
REHEARSAL
FOR THIS SHOW!

■

Most often, parents do the best job they can, given the information, experience, and tools at their disposal. The main problem is that there is no dress rehearsal for parenting. Once you have learned how to parent, the child is grown and the good as well as the damage is done. The legacy has again been passed on to the next generation. And so the cycle repeats itself, ad infinitum.

THE
INHERITANCE

■

But what is it that is passed on? What is so heinous that it would produce the condition called negaholism? What would make you feel that you couldn't be, do, or have what you wanted? What do parents do to engender negaholic children?

Parents from dysfunctional homes have a difficult time, since they have no positive model for effective parenting and are unable to break the chain which initially produced the condition within them.

Jill wanted to talk about her problems with her son, Scott. When he would do something that displeased her, she wouldn't raise her voice, get angry or talk to him, but rather would turn stone-cold. Fit, trim, the perfect yuppie, Jill looked as if she had just stepped off the tennis court.

"Every time Scott forgets to leave the dog outside, or leaves his wet towels on my best chintz upholstery, I get furious and then frozen. It's as if my blood runs cold and I can't speak. Something happens when I get angry, and for the life of me, I can't figure it out."

I asked Jill when this started.

"It's gotten worse the older he gets. Now it's gotten to the point where I'm genuinely concerned. It's not that I want to explode at him, but I get so blocked that I can't talk," Jill said, dismayed.

I asked her more questions. "What did your parents do when you had done something they didn't like?"

"Well, first my mother would scream and yell." Upon saying those words, Jill's face flushed and her eyes widened. She continued, "And then she would go stone-cold. She would run what I used to call her 'Frosty the Snowwoman,' which would go on for days. I'd have to beg her to talk to me. It felt like she'd taken her love away."

Jill's behavior patterning edited out her mother's yelling, but through the moth-eaten veil popped the "frostiness," which remained with her unconsciously. Jill then revealed her memory of her grandmother: a woman who would stay in her room for days and speak to no one.

THE SEVEN CHARACTERISTICS OF A DYSFUNCTIONAL FAMILY

■

The proper function of the family is to provide a healthy and supportive environment in which the members are encouraged to grow and develop individually and interpersonally into healthy, protective, and fully functional adults.

A dysfunctional family fails to fulfill its function. There are seven conditions which characterize a dysfunctional family, which I will discuss in the following pages.

LOVE IS CONDITIONAL

■

Diane had long, black, naturally curly hair, large green eyes like a cat's, and a wide, warm smile. She was constantly comparing herself with everyone.

"No matter what I do or what I achieve with my department in the hospital, I'm always comparing myself with the other nurses. I'm the head of the entire department, why am I comparing myself with my staff? Not only do I compare myself with my colleagues, I'm brutal with myself at the gym. Hell, I can be just walking down the street, and I hear this voice comparing myself to everyone around me. 'Look at her, she's so petite. You're so big; why, you'd make at least two of her. You might not be so bad if you lost, say, ten pounds, well, maybe fifteen. Look at those thighs. I can't believe that someone could wear a skirt that is so short. You could never wear a miniskirt like that. You'd look like a hippopotamus.'"

As we unraveled the past, Diane began to tell me about her relationship with her mother and her three older brothers. Her mother compared her unfavorably to her peers. She wasn't as cute as Kathy, as athletic as Anne Marie, as talented as Patricia, or as sweet and kind as Toni. Her brothers made fun of her for being awkward, and she felt like she could never measure up. In spite of her straight A's, she felt like a loser.

In a dysfunctional home, a measurement is established against which each member of the household is compared. The measurement can be different for each child. It could be academic achievement, malleability, obedience, compliance. Love is then given or withheld depending upon how each person measures up to the standard which has been set for him/her. The shoulds, musts, ought tos, supposed tos, have tos are the standards or rules which have been set by the parents (usually but not always unconsciously modeled after their own parents) and are the conditions under which love is dispensed.

THERE ARE TABOO TOPICS WHICH MUST NEVER BE ADDRESSED

The youngest child from a family of five, Dora was a petite redhead who wore her hair bobbed short and pulled over to one side. Dora couldn't talk to her husband about money. Every time they discussed the family budget, the children's education, or pension plans, her head would get all fuzzy, and she couldn't keep her thoughts straight. When I asked her about her childhood memories about money matters, she recounted that in addition to never being given an allowance, or having available cash, she couldn't remember her family ever having a discussion about money.

"Money seemed to pass through our lives, unseen by any of the children. It was like air: You knew it was there, but you couldn't see it. The cost of private school was never brought up, nor were any other costs related to daily living. I can't recall seeing a bill—or a check, for that matter. It all happened mysteriously. I never thought about money, since we never talked about it. I do remember hearing that Mommy had over-drawn her bank account, and Daddy wasn't pleased. Really the only money I ever saw was at the checkout counter at the grocery store. It wasn't that we were poor, far from it, we were quite well off, it was, well, one of those things that you just don't talk about."

Topics such as sex, religion, politics, money, relatives, ad-dictions, illnesses, feelings, interpersonal relationships, plans or activities, or the condition of a specific family member, are arbitrarily designated off-limits. Family members get the mes-sage either verbally or nonverbally that "we just don't talk about such things."

AN INABILITY TO DISCUSS, DEAL WITH, AND SUCCESSFULLY SOLVE ROOT FAMILY PROBLEMS

David was a hotelkeeper who was engaged to be married to Marge. He came under duress, since she had accused him of being cold and uncaring and unless he started to act toward her with more feeling, she threatened to break off with him. Tipping his chair back, his arms folded across his perfectly pressed designer jacket, David looked as if he had just stepped out of a fashion magazine.

"I don't know whether it's her or me, but I'm tired of being called cold and unfeeling. She thinks that since I'm not overly emotional like she is, there is something wrong with me. She overdramatizes everything, and gets hysterical at the drop of a hat. Maybe she is the one who has a problem. I need to be responsible for keeping some stability in the relationship, or she might go off the deep end. I've been through a lot, and not much fazes me. I've learned to keep my emotions under control, and that's what works in the business world."

"I understand, David. Can you describe the latest incident in which this issue came up?"

"Sure. We were talking about the future, buying a home, going away on our honeymoon, having children, and my response was that's fine. Everything is always fine. She says I have no emotions. All I ever say is 'no' or 'fine.' She gets so emotional; she seems to have enough emotions for the two of us combined."

"Would you mind telling me a little about the way emotions were handled in your family?"

"Don't mind at all. There weren't any!"

"What do you mean there weren't any?" I asked.

"My dad had a rare terminal illness that affects the central nervous system and gradually causes the nerves to deteriorate. As a result, the doctor cautioned my mom that there should be no display of emotion around him. That meant we couldn't get excited, sad, angry, or very happy anywhere within earshot. As a result, my sister and I learned to modulate all our feelings. There was no affection displayed, nor was there anger, love, or enthusiasm. We never talked about it; it was just how we had to live to keep Dad alive."

Problems can pertain to the family as a whole, to two or more family members and their interrelatedness, or to one member's nonfunctioning as it relates to the rest of the system. These are situations which are not discussed, are deliberately avoided, and dismissed when approached. Issues might involve such things as an illness, or the problems of a particular family member, eccentricities of one member or all, sibling rivalry, incest, money concerns, psychological conditions, or learning disabilities.

FAMILY SECRETS ARE GUARDED AND PASSED ON

Torrie had a problem she couldn't discuss. She was too ashamed and embarrassed to talk about it. She sat with arms and legs crossed, one leg swinging up and down nervously. She kept telling me what a wonderful life she had, and how happy she was. I told her that I was pleased and probed for the reason for the session. She said she had never told anyone her secret and didn't know if she could even bring herself to tell me, because she couldn't bear to talk about the subject. I explained that I was willing to help, and that whatever she said would be held in total confidence. If she wanted a therapist or a psychiatrist, I could refer her to someone with whom she might feel safer. She replied that she felt safe with me and that that wasn't the issue. She was going to deal with it today.

As she uncrossed her legs, she placed her elbows on her knees and looked down at the floor. "It's my mother. No it's not her, it's him. He did it. But she let it happen. It was one of them, or maybe it was all my fault. I don't know, but I can't look at him."

Gently I intruded into her monologue and asked, "Who?"

"My stepfather. He told her I made it all up. He said I lied, and I didn't. It happened. Then she accused me of pr-pr-provoking him. She didn't believe me. My own mother didn't believe me."

I finally got to the bottom of the issue and understood Torrie's confusion. Torrie was sexually abused when she was four years old. Her stepfather had molested her, and when she got up the courage to tell her mother, she was accused of lying, and then later of having provoked the incident. As a result, she was angry, hurt, shut down, and out of trust with her own inner self.

Torrie's situation with her stepfather is more common than one would suspect. In every self-esteem workshop that I lead there are always several women who have been sexually molested by a family member. At first I thought it was shocking, but it happens so frequently in so many well-off American homes that I now accept it with resignation, sadness, and my own quiet outrage. Torrie's secret became the family secret, which was guarded and passed on.

There is a common pact between all family members to

honor the code of silence regarding all family secrets. Secrets include family scandals, suicides, domestic violence, drinking problems, incest, money issues, any secret addictions, and/or eccentricities.

FEELINGS ARE DENIED, AVOIDED, DISCOUNTED, AND SUPPRESSED

Sabrina and Tim had a sixteen-year-old son who was giving them a lot of trouble. Robby was a normal teenager, testing his limits as he crossed the wobbly bridge between boyhood and manhood. Life progressed as usual, except that Sabrina and Tim had very different views on discipline. Sabrina believed that the best way to address a problem was to sit down and talk it through, while Tim held that the only way to get your point across was with punishment.

Sabrina was disturbed by the way Tim was treating Robby. "I think he is going to do some damage with that boy. It worries me," she said.

"How do you feel about the situation?" I asked.

"Just awful. But I simply don't know what to do about it."

"Have you told Tim how you feel about the way he disciplines Robby?" I probed.

"No. I can't talk to him about my feelings. He thinks I'm too soft and that I let Robby get away with murder. I feel caught between wanting to defend Robby and at the same time wanting to back Tim. I feel trapped and unable to do either. I tell myself it's none of my business, Tim needs to have his own relationship with his son, but it eats away at me every time they get into it. I try to shut it out, but I don't know what's right. What is the right thing to do as a mother?"

Feelings are perceived as dangerous. The expression of feelings is regarded as threatening, disruptive to the family system. It is met with disdain, rejection or, at best, tolerance. Strong emotion is often the impetus for action. Suppressing feeings preserves the situation, hence the status quo, and simultaneously creates an environment which is riddled with lies.

6

DENIAL IS A "NORMAL" CONDITION FOR THE FAMILY SYSTEM

∎

Lucy is the perfect model of the supermom. She is attractive, effective, organized, and charming. On top of all that, she is a terrific business executive. She came to me with the objective of resolving some issues in her marriage.

She said, "Roger is a good provider, a good father, and a good businessman, but sometimes little things make him irate. It scares me when he gets furious at me. Let me give you an example. When we go grocery shopping, he likes to push the cart. Please don't laugh at me when I tell you this—I know it's a small thing—but when I push the cart over to the shelves, he *insists* on holding it in place so that I can't budge it."

"Is he joking or teasing?" I asked.

"Oh no. He's dead serious. You see, it's this power struggle between us. He has to control the cart, and if I take hold of it, then he has relinquished the control. It's a metaphor for our entire relationship. God, I can't believe I'm telling you this, but last Friday night he got so mad at me that he put his elbow through the wall. Well, I was terrified and started crying. I get afraid just like I used to when I was little."

"What happened when you were little?" I nudged.

"My parents used to fight whenever they got drunk. They would yell and scream and throw things. I would crawl into bed with my sister and hide under the covers. You know, I never told any of my friends about my parents, and I don't want anyone to think bad thoughts about Roger."

* * *

Refusal to acknowledge what is true creates an environment that is riddled with inconsistencies, massive confusion, and uncertainty about what is, in fact, real. Denial of root problems leads to denial of ancillary issues, and then to suppression of any and all feelings related to the problem or the issues. The strategy is a blanket coverup, and the more feelings are suppressed, the more distorted, dishonest, unreal, and bizarre the situation becomes. In addition, you are supported in denying your perceptions, thoughts, and wants.

PRESERVATION OF THE FAMILY SYSTEM BY ALL CODEPENDENTS

Alice, an only child, thought that her job in life was to make peace between her parents. Alice is slight, with jet-black hair and shining eyes. She is the consummate peacemaker.

Alice explained her situation like this: "I always find myself making peace between two people. Now I am running over to my sister's house to make peace between her husband and her. I've just taken on this role, and I want to stop doing it. I want to let people work out their own problems, and stop meddling, or having to be needed, or whatever I do. I want to get out of my role and break the old way of operating. My problem is that I don't know any other way to behave. It's as if 'peacemaker' is a part of my very fiber, or part of my personality."

Each person has a specific role in the family, a role that exists to keep the family system in balance. Each person gives up his true self in exchange for a role which will keep the family intact. Each member of the codependent system has relinquished their true feelings and lives in reaction to the system's spastic movements. The closed system reinforces itself through the perpetuation of the myth, the lies, and the contrived scenario which is being perpetrated on all involved.

DYSFUNCTIONAL
FAMILIES
PRODUCE NEGAHOLICS
■

If you are a negaholic, the chances are that you came from a dysfunctional home in which at least three out of the seven conditions were present.

Negaholic compulsiveness is frequently triggered by stressful situations. Coping with stress, a product of modern times, is especially difficult for people who are raised in dysfunctional homes.

If you come from a dysfunctional home and you are a negaholic, don't despair: you are the norm, not the exception. You are among the majority, and, what's more important, if you keep your sense of humor, there is a route to sanity and a functional future.

In the next chapter you will see the relationship between stress and addictive behavior.

THREE

STRESS
AND
ADDICTIVE
BEHAVIOR

■

THE
TRAUMA
OF OUR
TECHNOLOGICAL
TIMES

■

Transportation, communication, and technology have turned the modern world upside down. Rapid pace, pressure, and ambiguity have changed our lives from being steady, consistent, and stationary to being fraught with confusion, disillusionment, and disconnection. The rhythm of the future brings rapid change, dramatic transitions, and traumatizing uncertainty. We are living in a turbulent, chaotic, and perplexing era. Never before in the history of mankind have there been so many options, with so few tools with which to cope.

TRUE
FALSE

Decidophobia

Time or Newsweek
2 or 3 yrs (or more) ago

WHAT
IS
STRESS?

■

Stress is a product of our times. It is something that we live
with every day. The way stress affects our lives is a new phenomenon. Think back to early rural America. Imagine a farmer
holding his hat in his hand, wiping his brow and saying "I'm
really stressed out!" It's hard to imagine, since life was so different then. This is not to say that the lives of people in those
days were easy, far from it, but it was a very different kind of
life from that we live today.

One hundred years ago, our ancestors didn't have the modern conveniences we have now, nor did they have the ad-
vances in transportation, communication, and technology.
They worked hard from sunrise to sunset. Their labor was
physical, and their worries related to their crops, the land, and
dealing with the elements. The roles of men and women were
clearly defined, and the options available to them were mini-
mal. They didn't have to figure out what career they wanted
to choose, or where they wanted to live. There weren't huge
controversies about what they should eat, their cholesterol
count, or how much fat, fiber, and sugar they should have in
their diet. Chemicals and their effect on health were not part
of their daily conversations. They weren't confronted with a
wide variety of cars to choose from, or new gadgets to buy, or
the option to travel anywhere in the world in mind boggling
mini-units of time. They didn't have to deal with issues such
as whether to get married or not, whether to have children
now, later, or ever. They probably didn't have to deal with the
stresses of relocating. They weren't mentally burdened with
the threat of nuclear war, AIDS, or cancer. Life was by no
means easy, but the pressures, concerns, and alternatives were
certainly different from what we know today. Their concerns
were more immediate, and "stress" did not exist.

the word

WHAT
PRODUCES
STRESS?

■

Since stress is a daily phenomenon of our times, let's examine some of the things that cause it.

- confusion and ambiguity about sex roles, expectations, and priorities
- role: confusion, conflict, overload, underload, either on the job or at home
- overglut and bombardment of options, from soap brands to sexual partners
- rapid pace, heavy demands, and the pressure of intense competition
- sensory assault from all angles, resulting in over-stimulation
- alienation resulting from the breakdown of the family, the church, and the community
- isolation resulting from high mobility, transience, and instability
- global financial instability with massive fluctuation in currencies
- the everpresent threat of termination from global war to epidemic diseases, which weigh heavily on our con-sciousness
- lack of time, lack of direction, frustration, and monotony
- physical pain or disability
- emotional traumas relating to family, loved ones, and friends
- changes: in lifestyle, economic status, marital status, educational status, career or job situation, increase or decrease in the family unit, relocation in home or job,
- baggage from growing up in a dysfunctional home in-cluding: feeling disconnected from our real feelings, being out of touch with our own personal wants, fear of

making mistakes, fear of taking risks, communicating, and being abandoned.

Is it any wonder we feel stressed? After all, what *is* stress? Stress is strain or force that taxes the system to such a degree that it begins to break down. In the human system, this means physical, emotional, psychological, interpersonal, or spiritual tension greater than the person can handle.

PD7PR

In effective self-management, you need to attend to the different aspects of yourself. You need to take a self-inventory to ensure that all the different parts of you are in good working order. (RESOURCES)

Since each person is unique, the degree of stress that each of us can handle is different. Where one person thrives on stress, another buckles at the thought of it. The process of managing stress is an individual concern. The problem, of course, is that most of us were never taught about stress, how to notice it before it becomes an issue, how to monitor it when it is a concern, and how to manage it when it has grown out of control. Being creatures of habit, we gravitate to what we know, to what is familiar. Our coping mechanisms are for the most part without thought, scrutiny, or conscious choice.

HABITS

The chart that follows is a graphic representation of the balance of input and output necessary to achieve equilibrium.

BALANCE

When you are able to maintain the balance of input and output, you are not overly stressed. Most of us were never taught self-management skills and we tend to ignore ourselves, as if we were machines that will go on running forever. We forget that if we don't attend to our well-being, we will get stressed, start acting even more compulsively, and reach out for temporary relief in order to cope with the day.

REACH OUT FOR TEMPORARY RELIEF

THE SELF CHART

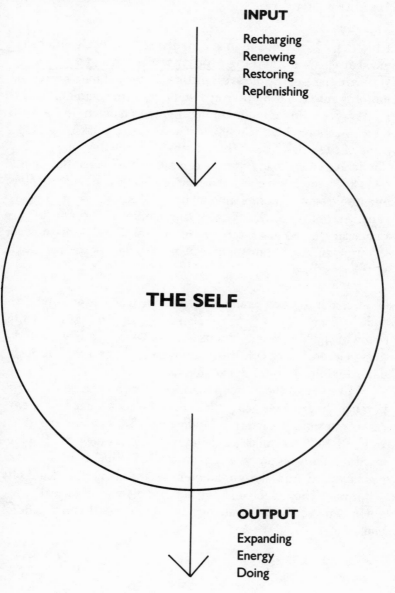

INPUT

Recharging
Renewing
Restoring
Replenishing

THE SELF

OUTPUT

Expanding
Energy
Doing

TEMPORARY
RELIEF
■

I like to call these coping mechanisms "mood alterators." A mood alterator is anything which instantly changes your mood. Here are some of the mood alterators that my clients have used: jumping into the pool, taking a walk, painting, screaming into a pillow, chewing gum, and jumping up and down. In her book *Quick Fixes & Small Comforts*, Dr. Georgia Witkin describes some of the little "fixes" that can help us get through the day. She labels them "behaviors"—coping mechanisms that enable us to keep going, give us a moment of pleasure, help to displace our unpleasant feelings, and/or indulge ourselves in some escape. According to Dr. Witkin, these "fixes and comforts" are temporary mood alterators, which act as Band-Aids to cover the problem for the moment, but never address the real issue at the core level.

Trish is a prime example of someone who has enjoyed little "quick fixes" as a way to cope with a busy and stressful life. Some of the "fixes" she has used have been: Fig Newtons, donuts, Oreo cookies, pralines-and-cream ice cream, Kit Kats, dates (edible ones), and protein shakes.

I like to call them cheap thrills rather than small comforts, because they always get you in the end. These wonderful treats can mysteriously turn into bludgeons. Unless you have given yourself 100% permission to indulge in the quick fix, the momentary high becomes a "cheap thrill." What may look like goodies turn into self-punishment, reinforcing the negaholic syndrome. They give you license to take yourself to task, they erode your self-trust, and they reinforce the "I can't" side of you.

THE
REESE'S
RUSH

Tall and lean, with straight brown hair cascading down her back, Trish's wide-set brown eyes focused intently on everyone she met. She reflected on the past and the onset of her compulsive behavior. Her theater background, plus cramming for exams, got her into the habit of reaching for fixes to get through the crunch. After all, it was just for the time being, or so she believed.

As she sat in the captain's chair by the window, twenty years after college, she leaned forward and confided in me that she was an addict. "I have become addicted to Reese's peanut butter cups," she said shyly.

This wasn't the first time Trish had indulged in mood alterators, so she wasn't seriously alarmed. "I know this is a tough time for me, with all the stress, so I'm indulging myself. It's only for a short time, until I get over the hump. This is hard, with no man in my life, and this crazy schedule—well, I just need some pleasure."

Trish found herself acting in an addictive way. She came to the realization that she couldn't get through the day without a Reese's peanut butter cup.

"I think about my Reese's all the time. I wonder, should I eat one early in the day, and save the other for evening, or should I eat them both together and get it over with? Maybe I should hide both cups until evening, then have them as a reward for getting my work done."

She saw herself sneaking around so that no one would see her gobbling down her Reese's. She couldn't eat them openly, since everyone knew she didn't eat sugar, and she didn't want to share her treat. She got so much pleasure out of those two little round cups that it reminded her of all those moments in childhood when she had been naughty. The adrenaline rush was the physical thrill of naughtiness.

GETTING
A KICK AND
GETTING KICKED
IN THE END

■

The child within was getting a kick out of being bad, but at the same time the adult who knows better was getting kicked for going against her belief system. She couldn't win for losing. She could control her craving to one Reese's per day, but after three weeks she started getting concerned.

"I can't stop the craving for Reese's. But then why should I? I mean it's not cocaine or heroin, it's just one Reese's a day. That's not all that bad, is it? A little naughtiness is healthy, after all. So much of my life is responsible, adult, and uptight. The Reese's rounds me out, it gives me depth," she said, justifying herself.   *the "interpreter" Gazzaniga (1985, 1988)*

The fact that she had lost control and was acting out of a nonrational craving was a sign that there was an imbalance. Inside her there was something missing that she was trying to fill with Reese's. She was feeling a sensation and wasn't coming to terms with her feelings.

She would argue, "I deserve it. I've been really good lately, a good employee, a good friend, and responsible to a fault. Hell, cutting loose with a Reese's is not going to kill anyone. I need to live a little!"

Everything her mind was telling her was accurate. It had assembled relevant and useful data to use at moments just like these. The point wasn't whether she was a good person, or whether she needed a reward, or whether the Reese's would kill her or not. The point wasn't whether she needed to be naughty, or whether she was allowing the child within to come out and play. The point was that she had lost control and needed to have a mood alterator to help her cope with the stresses of life. One bite of her Reese's and her mood was substantially altered.

She felt unloved and pressured, with no time to be able to get in touch with, feel, and process her feelings.

"One little Reese's," she said, "handles all my stress and anxiety in about five minutes for forty cents. How efficient, how effective, how economical. This is a good use of time, money, and energy. There is only one problem: I have become addicted."

As with all addictions, her desire would never stay the same; it would only grow until she would require greater quantities to satiate her need. She decided that this was the end of Reese's. What was more important for Trish was peeking underneath the behavior to understand what was really going on inside herself.

[handwritten right margin: potential myth — not true, in fact, she cut back to one.]

PEEKING UNDERNEATH THE BEHAVIOR

■

Underneath the behavior is a feeling. The feeling most often is undesirable, unacceptable, or unwelcome. The mood alterator is selected either to pursue or avoid the feeling. Since negaholics often come from a home environment in which feelings were avoided, denied, or suppressed, it is normal behavior to camouflage or distance yourself from feelings which are disturbing, disorienting, or distracting. To avoid such feelings by using mood alterators is a normal coping mechanism for our times. The situation gets dangerous when it hooks into negaholic behaviors; when the mood alterators become addictions used to further our self-flagellations—our negattacks. In other words, when you treat yourself to something that is bad for you in the long run, then repeat the behavior and use it as ammunition for the next personal war against yourself, you know you're in trouble.

Whenever mood alterators grow beyond your control they have become addictions. Addictions and stress are now a daily part of our lives. Addictions are a way to cope with stress. They are uncontrollable cravings for substances, activities, persons, places, and things which are compulsive, repetitious, involve loss of control, and are continued despite adverse consequences. Virtually anything or anyone can become an addiction.

[handwritten right margin: GACA ✕]

[handwritten bottom margin: What is gained/lost by such a broad interpretation?]

The addictive personality originates from the dysfunctional home.

Trish wanted to discuss her Reese's addiction. Since it was now a thing of the past, it was a good time for her to look underneath her addictive behavior, to try to understand it so that when the next attack struck she would be prepared.

TRIGGERS
OF HOW I
WAS SUPPOSED
TO BE

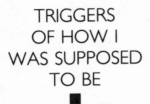

I asked Trish to describe her last bout with Reese's.

"I was at home talking on the phone with my best friend from college, Vickie," she said. "She talked about her two children, her husband, Garrett, and their beautiful home in New England. While she was talking, I began to feel a tightness in my stomach and a kind of reeling in my head. My own life started flashing before my eyes. I saw my three marriages, no children, a foreclosed home, and all my failures. It was more than I could stand."

"I remembered that I had stashed a Reese's in the cookie jar. I darted into the kitchen, reached for it, and for a moment got some instant relief," she said, with a deep sigh.

"Do you know why you got relief?"

"Well, I'm a chocoholic, maybe that's why," she responded.

"Yes, but you see there is something very specific about chocolate," I interjected. "You know how you feel when you're in love? Calm, soft, warm, and euphoric, as if you are in a dreamlike state?"

"I remember how that feels, but what does it have to do with Reese's?" she asked.

"There is a chemical in chocolate called phenylethylamine or PEA which affects the brain in almost exactly the same way that falling in love affects you. In other words, when you eat chocolate, you get the same calm, peaceful, dreamy feeling that you have when you first meet the man of your dreams," I explained.

WHERE DO ADDICTIONS ORIGINATE?

Trish's addiction is derived from an insufficient self-concept or image. The insufficiency manifests in various forms. For example, I'm not smart enough to do the task, not skilled enough to do the job, not attractive enough to have the relationship, not athletic enough to participate in the competition, not worthy enough to be really loved by a wonderful person, not thin enough, not sexy enough, not good enough, not powerful enough. The list could go on indefinitely, but the underlying feeling is that we aren't enough of something that we are supposed to be. This is the origin of the "I can't" person. Since the feeling of insufficiency is rarely addressed for what it is, and is often avoided, we pursue remedies to fill the void and alleviate the emptiness. In other words, we attack the symptom and not the root cause. The remedies are anything from Reese's to rum to running.

When you become addicted, you give away your power and become obsessed with something outside your self. You believe "it" is the solution to your problems. Your focus becomes increasingly external. "It" becomes the thing which makes you feel good, and solves the immediate stress at hand. As an addiction develops, you begin to see it as a panacea to life's problems and your behavior becomes increasingly compulsive. You eliminate other alternatives and become consumed by the addiction. When other people become concerned, critical, or meddlesome, you deal with their responses to your behavior by camouflaging your activities. You start with vagueness, then evolve to mild cover-ups, and finally escalate your deception so that you are telling out-and-out lies.

THE
ADDICTIVE
PERSONALITY
TRAITS

There are commonalties which people share who are under stress, come from dysfunctional homes, and are addicted to something. People who are under a lot of stress, who try to cope with the stress by using mood alterators, and who have a tendency to become addictive have frequently been raised in dysfunctional homes. The ten addictive personality traits are:

1. Type "A" personality: Driven, ambitious, competitive, hard-driving
2. Impulsive: sensation-seeking, exploratory and a risk-taker
3. Compulsive: overly orderly, perfectionistic, and conscientious in the performance of activities
4. Quick-tempered, excitable, and irascible
5. Self-confident, uninhibited, energetic, and hyperactive
6. Rigid in thinking: a binary approach to life
7. Extremely sensitive to pain, as well as susceptible to physical anxiety
8. High novelty-seeking and low harm-avoidance
9. Sentimental and moody, with a propensity toward mood swings
10. Dependent on extrinsic rewards for self-validation: wealth, power, possessions, prestige, social acceptance

You need not possess all these traits to be an addictive personality. The ones given above, however, are those most commonly found in addictive behavior.

There are two types of addictions, according to Anne Wilson Schaef, author of *When Society Becomes an Addict*. She makes a distinction between substance addiction and process addiction. When people are addicted to artificially refined products which are consumed, they are called *"substance"* addicts. These substances include alcohol, drugs, nicotine, caffeine, sugar, and food in general, and can be related to such abuses as overeating, anorexia, and bulimia. They are almost always mood-altering, and lead to increased physical dependence. On the other hand, people who get hooked on a process, a specific set of actions or interactions, are known as *process* addicts. Obsessions with making money, gambling, sex, relationships, working, daydreaming, worrying, television, exercise, shopping, and even self-help programs are categorized as process addictions.

Take Sam for instance. Sam is a negaholic and a process addict. His addiction is daydreaming, which fits into his negaholic pattern by giving him a weapon to use on himself. Sam became addicted to daydreaming as a way to escape the pain and boredom of daily living. Why did this happen? Sam's father was a fundamentalist minister, and he was raised in a religious home. All responsibility was allocated to God or the devil. Sacrifice was highly valued, as were self-denial and asceticism. To pursue your own wants and worldly desires was considered the devil's work. Daydreaming and fantasizing were Sam's ways of escaping from this repressive, unstimulating, and punitive existence. He would fantasize about writing wonderful novels, having exciting, beautiful women, fast cars, and being a famous personality.

When he was eighteen, Sam was sent to a seminary from which he was expelled after a year for not obeying the rules. He rebelled against what he had learned from early childhood, the standards by which one should live. Another part of him still fantasized about worldly desires, and he would feel guilt and despair about this. He would think to himself, "I will never have the money, homes, cars, clothes, friends, degrees, and art that I want." Why did Sam drift from his cocoonlike world of daydreaming into mental negaholism? Eventually, Sam recognized the internal schism within himself, and it became his self-torment. He became addicted to tormenting himself both for not being a true minister's son, and for never being able to be, do, or have what he wanted.

He would be hard on himself so that he

- would atone for his worldly ways
- would get an internal rush
- would feel justifiably punished rather than despairing
- would feel something exciting even if it was self-punitive

THE KEY ELEMENTS WHICH UNDERLIE ALL ADDICTIVE BEHAVIOR
■

Whether you are a negaholic who is addicted to daydreaming, dogs, or drugs, there are certain characteristics which underlie all addictive behavior. [nine(9)]

IMMEDIATE GRATIFICATION. All addictions produce instant gratification. You feel better as a result of your involvement with the substance or process in which you indulge. It is enjoyable to experience the altered state (at least temporarily).

SIMPLISTIC THINKING. You believe that "it" will make everything all right. You believe that "it" is a panacea capable of inducing positive psychological, emotional, and physical states, as well as relieving negative ones.

DISTORTED PRIORITIES. Your priorities become distorted, and you become consumed and obsessed with your addiction as the most important thing in life, above and beyond everything else.
reduced integrative capacity

SKEWED PERSPECTIVE. Your perspective becomes skewed and inaccurate. You are unable to perceive reality accurately. You begin to see people and situations as exaggerations of what they normally are.

Gazzaniga — Stress - focus on #1 priority -
BUT is #1 priority the most relevant and
critical to the situation at hand ?

SYMPTOMS OF WITHDRAWAL. As soon as you are deprived of the substance or the process, adverse consequences appear immediately. You experience unpleasant physiological, psychological, and/or emotional symptoms. You experience trauma at the thought or reality of separating from your addiction.

OVERWHELMING ATTACHMENT. You are so dependent upon the addiction that you feel unable to function without it. A need/dependency relationship evolves between you and your addiction. You need it to be happy and your well-being is contingent on having it available to you.

COMPLETE LOSS OF POWER. You feel powerless to alter your situation. You have relinquished your power to something or someone outside yourself. The situation has become bigger than you are, and you are unable to affect a change. You are a slave to your addictions.

BINARY THINKING. You are a victim of binary thinking. You view situations as black or white, either/or, right or wrong, good or bad, on or off, wonderful or awful. Life is perceived as a zero sum game in which the pendulum swings between two polar opposites with no happy medium.

PROGRESSIVE AND CONSISTENT STAGES OF INVOLVEMENT. You need greater quantities of the addictive substance to satisfy the need within. You have built up a natural immunity, and in order for your addiction to have an impact, you need increasing exposure. These stages include initial use, continuation of use, transition from use to abuse, cessation, control of abuse, transference to another addiction, and, in three-quarters of the cases, relapse.

We all have addictions of varying degrees. To some extent, we could all be called addicts. The reason is that we live in an addicted society. Think for a minute. Who do you know who isn't addicted to something? It might not be life-threatening, but do you know anyone who isn't addicted to sugar, caffeine, cigarettes, worrying, or exercise?

Everywhere you turn in society, there is encouragement, which reinforces the premise of insufficiency. There is always a promise of an answer residing in an external solution that will solve all immediate problems. These problems may be tension, anxiety, stress, depression, headaches, constipation, poor self-image, lack of sex appeal, rejection by peers, traumatic love relationships, or whatever, but the advertising which bombards us daily tells us that there *is* an answer—you can buy it, feel better, and get relief, if only temporarily. Addictive behavior is when a person forms an attachment to something and believes that his well-being is contingent upon its perpetuation.

Addictions by definition are self-destructive. They erode self-esteem and cause gradual health problems, and impairments in social, occupational, physical, emotional, or spiritual functioning. In a sense, all addictions are displays of negaholism. Our society condones addictions.

So much of the social fabric of everything we do involves the acceptance of addictive thinking and behavior that we have become almost unaware of it.

WHY DO YOU BECOME ADDICTED?

Over the years, a series of different theories have developed concerning the origin of addictive behavior. The most traditional one suggests that the individual is lacking in willpower or moral character, and is unable to control his behavior. The second theory presents addiction as an illness. This theory removes the moral, judgmental stigma previously associated with addictive behavior. It releases the addicted person from personal responsibility and enables him to seek treatment without embarrassment or humiliation.

The biological theory regards addiction as evolving from

a genetic, metabolic, or biochemical disorder. From this perspective all addictions are viewed as physiologically based. The final theory proposes that addiction is a behavioral issue. Addictions are seen as learned behaviors, the result of past experiences and current circumstances. This theory presumes that everyone has power over his own destiny, and suggests that each person can control his behavior if he learns how to modify it.

All these theories are valid in their own right. No one theory is valid exclusively, but all are interdependent. There are an abundance of case studies which justify each theory. None of them are mutually exclusive.

The one underlying factor which binds them together is the opiate peptides, B-endorphins, B-lipotropin, and enkephalin. These substances, which are naturally secreted in the body, create a natural high, a feeling of euphoria. This feeling is addictive. Whether it is naturally induced or chemically induced, the result is the same: relief from anxiety, peace, well-being, and a temporary experience of complete and total euphoria. *This feeling is addictive.*

Now we get to the curious part: How does self-negation relate to euphoria? If you are a negaholic, every time you criticize, judge, or invalidate yourself, you release the same opiate peptides that you release when you take drugs or run. The rush that you feel when you punish yourself is an exciting *negative* feeling. People want to stop beating themselves up, but, in fact, they feel unable to do it. Why? They are addicted to the opiate peptides that allow them to feel this rush of excitement.

Let's take an example. You are late once again for an appointment and you hear, "I can't believe you're late! You should have left earlier. You knew what time you should have left, and you blew it. He is probably going to leave, and it will take months to get another appointment with him. He is going to be standing around waiting for you, and you're not there. How inconsiderate of you. You really have no concept of time. You're always late. You'll probably blow the whole deal. After all the work you have put into this deal, and now you go and screw it up by being late. You idiot! Can't you do anything right? Maybe you should get out of this line of business, since you can't manage your time. You're hopeless!"

Now let's explore the feelings you have just felt while reading this.

- Did it sound familiar?
- In the past, have you heard a voice in your head talking to you in this way about something you did or didn't do?
- Does this happen repeatedly with some item?
- Has it happened more than three times with the same situation?

You may have identified with it, heard some similarities, but stop for a minute and notice your feelings. Did you feel anything? If you felt something, what was it? Tune in and notice.

You may have felt a sensation in your chest—constriction, pressure, heat, a rush, increased heart rate.

Did you feel important?
Were you getting a lot of attention (albeit negative)?
Did you feel self-consumed?
Were you preoccupied with your situation, your plight, your drama?
Did you feel like the leading man or woman in your movie (soap opera)?
Did you feel bad yet, in a strange way, almost good, all at the same time?

The obvious conclusion would be never to be late again and thereby avoid the cycle of self-punishment forever. But the reality of the situation is that you, who have just been mean to yourself, have successfully reinforced all of the behaviors that you wanted to eliminate. You probably *will* be late again, maybe even habitually.

You have just acted out negaholism. You acted in a self-sabotaging manner. You tormented yourself mercilessly for something which was not a capital offense. You behaved in an

stingy with self-endorsement

addictive way in that you were unable to control your actions; you were powerless in the situation; your priorities became distorted; your perspectve became skewed; you had a sense of immediate gratification and you were unable to stop the behavior at will. You experienced the opiate peptides. The adrenaline rush was in full force. This is self-destructive behavior, and you will continue to perpetuate it, not because you want to, but because you cannot stop it. You are addicted!

Your obvious comment is: "Yeah, but being hard on yourself is not a euphoric state. How do you explain that?"

Physiologically speaking, "being hard on yourself" is not in and of itself a euphoric or desirable state, but the feeling that is created as a result of the release of opiate peptides like enkephalin, a pituitary hormone which is released into the blood, is the same as the endorphins which one experiences when running. The preoccupation with self, the feeling of self-consumption, self-importance, and the huge amount of attention (even though negative) you receive creates a state which feels wonderfully awful, deliciously disgusting, ecstatically agonizing. Self-flagellation is the ultimate oxymoron.

To *feel* is to experience being alive; to feel the life force coursing through your veins. To feel and experience *anything* means that you are not dead. So you run into a situation in which you are at cross-purposes: Part of you does anything in your power not to feel, since feelings have been labeled forbidden, while the other part of you is longing to feel something, anything, in order to confirm the fact that you are alive.

The insufficiency, emptiness, and deep-seated feelings of inadequacy, fear, and loneliness which are rooted deeply in your self-concept are satiated and validated every time the mean mechanism clicks into gear. It is as if the reaction of self-cruelty is an appropriate response to your lack of self-worth. The self-punishment is seen as a kind of atonement for the "wrong doing" that the person has perpetrated simply by existing. Taking yourself to task forces you to toe the line and behave properly in the future. This backfires, since the negativity only reinforces the pattern.

When you grow up in a dysfunctional home, and as a result

have a low self-concept, you draw to you a negativity that reinforces your self-image and gives you the ammunition with which to hurt yourself. Every time you do this, you restimulate the rush of opiate peptides which give you the feeling of self-importance and attention. The more you negate yourself, the more negative attention you receive, the more you are addicted to feeling bad, being negative, and reinforcing your nega-holism.

Feelings play a key role in transcending your negaholism. In Chapter Four, you will see why feelings are so important, and what you can do about them.

FOUR

TO
FEEL
OR NOT
TO FEEL

■

That really is the question. You need to ask yourself, "Am I willing to start feeling?" Of course you might say, "I do feel. I cry at movies. I get angry in traffic. I empathize with my friends. I love my cat." Yes, you feel to a degree, but what I'm talking about is a little different. I'm talking about a way of life which is committeed to experiencing, communicating, and expressing your feelings. Specifically, it means being painfully honest. It doesn't mean brutally honest, it means honoring your own reality.

BARBARA'S
BREAKTHROUGH
■

A client of mine named Barbara had fallen in love with a man named Jerry. They had been seeing each other, making plans for the future, and generally having a lot of fun. One night, Jerry took out Barbara's roommate without telling Barbara. One thing led to another, and they ended up spending the night together. Barbara was devastated. In our session, she admitted her feelings to me. She felt humiliated, hurt, and embarrassed beyond belief. She had really fallen for Jerry, and she was beating herself up for caring so much about him. She was very upset and on top of that she was angry at herself for being so upset. She didn't want to feel all the feelings that had surfaced. They spanned the spectrum from hurt to rage, from loss to revenge, from a sense that she was being victimized to apathy. None of these feelings were desirable to her; they exposed her and left her vulnerable to criticism and still more hurt. She wanted to cut off the feelings, and be a rock, impenetrable and strong.

She considered lying and admitting that she never cared that much about Jerry in the first place, that he didn't matter to her, that it was only a casual affair anyway, and she was searching for the part of her that could actually say all this. She thought that if she was aloof and unemotional she could distance and protect herself from the situation.

I probed. "What do you want, Barb? Are you willing to feel?"

She argued for all the reasons *not* to feel. She explained that when her friends had gone to Jerry and confronted him about his behavior toward her, he had said that what was between them was no big deal, and she was the one who was making such a big thing out of it. Barbara's friends, in turn, asked her why she was so upset. Since Jerry had said it was no big deal, why was *she* making such a fuss? In order to save face with her friends and deflect the embarrassment, she was seriously considering stifling her feelings, lying about her real inner truth, and getting on with her life.

I reminded Barb that the choice was up to her, and I asked her in the long run what would really serve her. She broke down and said, "I don't want to walk around like a human puddle. If I let myself feel, I may never stop crying. Then I'll be no good to anyone. Why did I let myself fall in love with him anyway, when he didn't even care about me? What kind of jerk am I?"

I asked her if she could be just a little gentler on herself. Falling in love with someone is not the worst thing in the world, even if it is unrequited. I asked her if she could permit herself to have fallen in love with a man who didn't love her back, to feel all the feelings which were her real truth right now, and to let herself be a vulnerable, caring human being. She thought about it, and let me know that it would be difficult, but that she would try.

The choice for Barbara was whether to feel and honor her inner truth regardless of what it was, or to save face, cut off the feelings, be strong and cold and tough. She weighed the pros and cons carefully before she chose. Barbara chose to take the risk of being human. This was a turning point in her life. She made a deliberate choice to feel and honor her inner truth rather than be cool and behave in an acceptable manner. This was a breakthrough for Barbara.

CEIL'S CHOICE

■

The choice which faced Barbara was not unique. Ceil had a similar one to make. When her mother died, she had had to handle all the details—the funeral arrangements, the disposal of personal effects, the affairs of the estate. There was so much that had to get done over a short period that she didn't want to take the time to feel. She thought that her time would be better used if she was goal-oriented. She felt that she needed to be resourceful and focus on tasks. She did not *process* her feelings by feeling them, allowing them to be, and releasing them. She put a lid on her grief, loss, sadness, hurt, anger, and abandonment, and held them all tightly within herself.

Years later Ceil sat in my office wondering why she had difficulty feeling joy. She had lost her spark somewhere on the road of life and she couldn't get it back. Now she again had a choice. Did she want to start feeling, to give herself permission to be a real human with legitimate feelings, and claim her right to have and to release them? Or did she want to be just an efficient, task-oriented machine?

Ceil had been stifling her feelings for so long that the situation looked completely overwhelming. She was afraid that she would have to take each situation from childhood on, and go through them one at a time experiencing the feelings. I let her know that she didn't need to quit her job and make this her life's work, but rather to make the choice to feel moment to moment as her feelings surfaced. Relieved, she was willing to consider "one moment at a time" as her new motto.

DON'T ROCK THE BOAT

■

There are a variety of reasons not to feel. Our society frowns on expressing feelings, and those who are emotional are regarded as weak, unprofessional, or self-indulgent. One client of mine felt that if she allowed her feelings to show and addressed them, she would rock the boat.

I asked her what she meant, and she said, "It's much easier to go along with whatever is being said or done rather than speak my own truth. So often my feelings are out of step with what is happening around me that if I spoke up I would be making messes everywhere."

Another told me, "I don't really trust my feelings, so when I feel something funny—you know, in my stomach—I think I'm crazy or like something's wrong with me."

Others think feelings take too long, are too messy, are too painful, aren't worth the bother. Some are afraid of what others will think, and still others are living out the fantasy picture of our perfect TV families.

FEELING
LEFT OUT
HURTS JUST AS
MUCH AS IT USED TO
■

Mary was self-employed and had two female partners. They were all very close until some problems in the business started to surface. Mary was constantly irritated with Dee Dee, one of her partners. She was finding fault with everything Dee Dee did, criticizing her suggestions and judging her actions. Mary wanted to figure out why she was so upset with Dee Dee.

In our session, we started tracking back in time to find the point at which things had changed. We explored the recent past and the more distant past and hit on an important clue. Until the fall things had been just great, and then everything started to get strange.

I asked what had happened in the fall, and Mary couldn't remember. We looked through her date book and reviewed the month of November day by day. Lo and behold, November was the month that Dee Dee got married. I asked Mary if this was important, and she said, "I didn't get invited to the wedding." I asked if she had expected to be invited.

She said that it was a small wedding, only the family was invited, and Dee Dee had told her this, but her feelings *were* hurt. She felt left out. I asked her if she ever told Dee Dee how she felt, and she replied, "No, I was too embarrassed to bring it up. What Dee Dee did was understandable, and I was acting childish."

I pointed out that that incident, small though it may seem, might be the withheld communication which had started all Mary's problems. A seed was planted that would later bear poisonous fruit.

FEELINGS
ARE NOT
THOUGHTS
◼

Feelings and thoughts are different. Thoughts, by definition, are rational, reasonable, and logical. Feelings are not rational, reasonable, or logical. To try to make sense out of your feelings is like trying to get cream from cabbage. By the same token, feelings are not right or wrong, they just are. We spend so much time and energy trying to figure out what our feelings mean, whether they are right, logical, or make sense, when the real truth about feelings is that they *don't* make sense. Childish misunderstandings and miscommunications happen every day. People get hurt, sad, angry, and upset all the time. That is not the issue. The real issue is how we deal or don't deal with our feelings.

CREATIVE
CASE-BUILDING
◼

Tim and Jay worked together in the same company, Tim was responsible for sales and Jay was responsible for the service department. There had been problems between the two departments, and a cold war had polarized them into two separate camps. As a consultant to the company, it was my task to see if there wasn't a way to bring all parties together, figure out what the issues were, and try to resolve them.

In the meeting, some interesting things began to surface. We started digging back in time to when things went bad, and came upon an incident which had occurred six months earlier.

Sales finally landed an account they had been working on for almost two years. When it got passed to the service department, some problems were mishandled and the account went sour. The problematic situation then backfired to the sales department. Tim was furious and tried to get Jay on the phone.

Jay was out of town, in meetings, and busy putting out other fires. The account was a priority for Tim, but unfortunately it wasn't for Jay.

Tim decided that the service department didn't care about the sales department, nor did service care about the customer. Tim started making offhand comments about the service department which his staff picked up on and this added fuel to the fire. The schism between sales and service grew and grew until the tension could be felt by all.

In our session, Tim uncovered and disclosed his feelings of anger, hurt, frustration, and hopelessness. We unearthed the initial incident and started to repair the damage from the past so that the two departments could cooperate and collaborate once more.

This is not an uncommon situation. You react to situations constantly: Actions are taken, things happen, and you react. It is normal to react. If you didn't react, there would be something wrong with you. You respond or react because you are a human, feeling person. Feelings are an integral part of being human. It is how you deal with your feelings that is critical. In this particular situation, the feelings were internalized instead of being dealt with. If we dissect the situation between Tim and Jay, it looks something like the case-building chart on the next page.

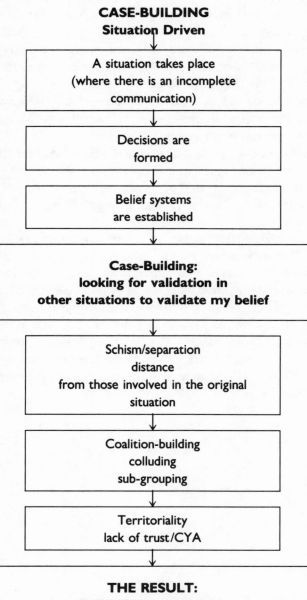

CASE-BUILDING
Situation Driven

A situation takes place
(where there is an incomplete
communication)

Decisions are
formed

Belief systems
are established

Case-Building:
looking for validation in
other situations to validate my belief

Schism/separation
distance
from those involved in the original
situation

Coalition-building
colluding
sub-grouping

Territoriality
lack of trust/CYA

THE RESULT:
Self-fulfilling prophesies

An incident occurs which causes feelings, which are unresolved. These feelings are turned into a judgment, next a decision is made, then a belief system is formed. Ultimately, a self-fulfilling prophesy perpetuates itself forever unless circumvented. In this situation,

- Tim's long-anticipated sale backfired. His expectations were unfulfilled.
- He felt anger, hurt, frustration, and hopelessness.
- He tried to contact Jay with no results.
- He judged Jay as unavailable.
- He decided that Jay didn't care about him, or the sales department, or making sales for the company.
- He formed the belief that the service department didn't care about the sales department, nor did they care about the customers—that, as a matter of fact, service was only there to collect their paychecks, they didn't care about anything but money. The entire sales department started to mirror Tim's feelings and beliefs and started to think that all the service department were useless good-for-nothings.

The sales department had a general attitude toward the service department that was riddled with feelings of malice, with judgments ranging from incompetence to distinterest. Yet few of them could tell you where these feelings and judgments came from. Their response would be, "Everyone knows that service is . . ."

Tim was willing to look within himself to sort out what his feelings were. It was a risky situation, because people often think that talking about feelings in a business environment is not appropriate. In order to get the venom out of the festering wound we had to go right into the center of the hurt feelings and dig out the poison.

And so a simple misunderstanding becomes silences, coalitions, armed camps, and, eventually, a full-blown cold war.

BAROMETERS
AND
SIGNALS
■

Feelings control your attitudes, moods, and sense of well-being.
They are natural expressions of your internal condition. Feelings are a measure of your reality. They are the barometers
that tell us whether someone is an ally or an adversary;
whether something is desired or rejected; whether to halt or
proceed. Feelings are pivotal to the physical, mental, and emotional health of every human being.

FEELINGS
ARE
PURPOSEFUL
■

Feelings are fundamental to the negaholic recovery. Sorting
out, acknowledging, expressing, and communicating feelings
are essential to the health of every organism, every person,
family, or organization. Dealing with the innermost feelings
in an honest and straightforward manner is fundamental to
the health and proper functioning of any entity.

Feelings exist to orient and reorient you to yourself and
your world. They connect you with your inner truth regardless
of whether it is "right" or "wrong." They also integrate you
with your essential self. By allowing and releasing your feelings, you become free to live life fully. Your feelings give you
immediate feedback regarding your relationship with yourself
and others. Your sense of well-being with yourself has greater
impact on your happiness and fulfillment than anything else,
and it is feelings that give you important information about
your condition and well-being.

WHEN
YOU PLAY
HOOKY ON
YOUR FEELINGS
∎

When feelings are not dealt with, they become bottled up and create a blockage—personally and *inter*personally. This, in turn, isolates you from yourself and your world. The fastest and surest way to become detached from reality is to avoid, discount, discredit, and suppress the real emotions that connect you to your core. Remember that in Chapter One we said that the core feelings of a negaholic are inadequacy, fear, and loneliness. If these feelings are never dealt with and released, then the only recourse is the pursuit of a sense of well-being through any means possible, even if it means engaging in activities that are self-destructive. In other words, if you are cut off from your feelings, and you need to feel in order to confirm the fact that you exist, you will strive to feel something. Most people would prefer to feel something desirable as opposed to something undesirable, but, given the choice, they would opt to feel something, even though unpleasant, over feeling nothing.

DESIGNER
FEELINGS
∎

Some people try on feelings as if they were clothes. They check them out to see if they like them or not. If they want them, then they may be incorporated into their wardrobe of feelings. They use their analyzing skills to assess desirability. They also try to categorize their feelings into good and bad. They distinguish happiness, joy, pleasure, and peace as "good" feelings, which are acceptable and desirable. They label anger, sadness, hurt, depression, and pain as "bad" or undesirable emotions. Then they try to have some and disallow others. This is difficult if not impossible to do.

Feelings are all tied up together. If you allow yourself to have your feelings, then you must allow *all* feelings. If you suppress your feelings, then you suppress *all* feelings. You can't selectively say "I'll keep joy, but get rid of depression," or "I'll never be lonely again, but let's let in all the pleasure that's possible." It just doesn't work that way. Feelings are woven together in a big interconnected web. The web is loosely enough knit so that if you suppress anger, you don't necessarily totally suppress passion, but tightly enough knit so that if you keep your anger in check, you can never completely let your passion fly. The point of choice is to feel or not to feel.

FEELINGS ARE THE LIGHTS ON THE DASHBOARD OF LIFE

All feelings are equally valid and necessary. They are like the oil, gas, and other lights on the dashboard of a car—indicators telling you that something is happening inside the engine. When you are running low on gas, a light goes on to indicate that you need to fill up. You could respond in several ways. You could be pleased that the light is working and that you will know about the problem ahead of time and take proper measures so that you aren't left stranded somewhere. You could be upset because you don't have time to get to a gas station or because your car uses up so much gas, or because you just got gas and whoever used your car last didn't refill it. Or you could be upset because the cost of gas these days gets you hot under the collar; when you were young it cost so much less. Or you could be mad because you just don't like the idea that cars need gas to run. On the other hand, you could ignore the lights on your dashboard altogether and see what happens.

TELL ME/
I DON'T
WANT TO KNOW
■

Some people are pleased to have an indicator to tell them what is going on and let them deal with it properly. Other people are annoyed by the very fact that they have feelings. They think of them as an unnecessary nuisance, a bad use of their time, and messy as well. They may deem them inappropriate and irksome and something they would be much better off without. Still other people avoid and ignore their feelings until the organism comes to a complete halt. Much like the car running out of gas, the human organism will shut down—will have a nervous breakdown, burnout, or a heart attack—when the red light indicators are consistently ignored.

RELIEF
IS JUST A
PUFF, BITE,
ZZZZZZ AWAY
■

Recall the situation with Sarah, in Chapter One, who had a fight with her man, had a sick cat, who wasn't feeling good, but wasn't really aware of her true feelings. She was embarrassed to admit the ones she was most in touch with, and as a result she suppressed them. Watch what happens to Sarah after she decides to get "fast relief." In the first scenario, Sarah wants to feel better. Like most people in our society, she wants relief fast, like the antacid commercials tell us. She wants to feel better instantly, if possible. She doesn't want to experience any discomfort or the feelings associated with her situation. Her first thought is to have a cigarette. Next she thinks of having some chocolate ice cream. Her third thought is "I wonder what is on TV?"

When you observe this behavior, it appears normal. But let's return to Sarah and examine her solution.

THE GAME OF "GOTCH YA"

■

After considering the alternatives, Sarah chooses all three: cigarettes, ice cream, and TV. The result is she feels sedated, calm, and peaceful. For the time being she experiences enough pleasure and distraction to eclipse the undesirable feelings.

When the sitcom on TV finishes, a wave of loneliness and sadness pass over her. She thinks to herself, "You never should have eaten that ice cream. You have no willpower. You're so fat! And at this rate you're only going to get fatter."

A justifying, nurturing voice might say, "Wait a minute, you needed that little bit of pleasure; besides it wasn't *that* much ice cream. After all you've been through, you deserve it." The critical retort might be, "You're so weak. You said you wanted to stop smoking, yet, at the slightest provocation, you go directly for the cigs. You're pathetic!" "Hey, why don't you go watch some more TV and take your mind off things." The rebuttal: "You are nothing but a couch potato! All you do is run to the TV to escape reality. Now start facing your problems!"

Sarah feels a rush inside from this internal self-attack. She feels a strange simultaneous mixture of excitement and depression. She is confused about her feelings, but she can't stop hurting herself. She is caught in the mental negaholic trap: the self-inflicted mental harangue. She punishes herself for many reasons:

- it carries on a tradition established by a loved one, usually in childhood
- it has become a habit, and as such is very familiar

- it creates a sense of self-absorption and self-importance, which can be very gratifying
- it creates a feeling like an internal rush, which is exciting
- it gives the person a lot of attention, which is rewarding even though it is negative, especially if attention is lacking elsewhere in her life

SOCIETY
LOOKS
DOWN ITS NOSE
■

In our current society, feelings are ignored, discounted, invalidated, and/or repressed. We are taught repeatedly that our feelings are not legitimate and should not be trusted. We have been led to believe that feelings should be denied and avoided, and that expressing them will only get us into trouble. We are indoctrinated to believe that feelings are wrong and disruptive, and this belief is reinforced through disapproval, avoidance, and punishment. From a very young age the learning process teaches us to disassociate or to disconnect from our innermost feelings, to learn not to feel and to intellectualize.

When feelings occasionally erupt at a movie, an altercation with a loved one, or at a ritual (a birth, marriage, or death), we feel momentarily out of control and immediately need to regain control. We suppress the threatening feelings. Suppressing feelings becomes such a conditioned response that after a short time it is automatic. If you are disconnected from your feelings you have an opportunity. You are at a crossroads: You can continue to engage in the old behavior, or you can start feeling your feelings.

For the most part the mind is connected to the old pattern, the addictive behavior, and the feelings are totally bypassed. You don't feel, you don't think to feel, you don't instinctively examine your feelings, your all-consuming need is to get relief.

You are not able to change the negative behavior and pursue healthier alternatives to wholeness the minute your feelings are awakened. You have just become aware of your feelings; you are as yet without the skills to implement change. This stage is potentially the most frightening and disruptive because you have the awareness but not the behavorial change. This schism creates guilt, remorse, and self-flagellation. Though this state is on the path to recovery, it feels the farthest from it. It is like hitting bottom before reconnecting with your essential self. One of the blocks to owning your feelings is embarrassment.

EMBARRASSMENT REIGNS AND TERRORIZES
■

As adults, feelings are often perceived as embarrassing. To feel hurt, sad, angry, or even jealous is exposing a vulnerable part of our humanity. To let others know that we are human, that we feel, that we care enough to feel intensely is inherently embarrassing. There are some feelings which are considered so unacceptable, so heinous that people won't dare admit having them. Anger at a coworker who has been promoted over you, jealousy of a sibling who just received public acclaim, hurt about not being invited to a friend's party are examples of some of the feelings which one might be reluctant to admit.

THE FIVE STEPS TO THE SUCCESSFUL MANAGEMENT OF EMOTIONS
■

What do you do with these feelings? How do you deal with them? Feelings can run your life or you can take charge and manage them. They can terrorize you so that, as a defense, you completely suppress them. Or they can flair up at any time when you least suspect them, making you look out of control. You need to know how the feelings can be identified, sorted out, and dealt with in healthy and appropriate ways. The more acquainted you are with your feelings, the easier it is to handle them when they surface. The more you ignore them, the more they control and dictate your behavior.

1) SORTING OUT THE FEELINGS

There is rarely one isolated feeling which is lingering all by itself, but rather an assortment of feelings all tangled together and intertwined, much like spaghetti. The sorting-out process means getting hold of each strand of spaghetti separately, holding it, feeling it, letting it be without judgment, and assigning it a name. This process is reflective and introspective. It requires patience, and quiet time. It is often advisable to have a person there helping to draw out, separate, and label the different pieces. Sorting out is also called "getting in touch with yourself," or "knowing what is going on with you."

2) ACKNOWLEDGING YOUR FEELINGS

After all the feelings are sorted out comes the moment when the truth is told. Admitting that your feelings are yours, owning them as your reality without having to justify, explain, or understand them is the next essential step in the process.

3) EXPERIENCING, EXPRESSING, AND RELEASING YOUR FEELINGS

Often people think that once they have sorted out and acknowledged their feelings it's all done; they can get back to everyday life. It's not as easy as that. In order for healing to take place effectively, there needs to be a release. It's as if you wanted to have a wound heal, but you left the venom inside. You need to extract the poison before the healing can take place. Emotionally speaking, the poison is the feeling(s) that you have been harboring within yourself. That feeling needs to be released in order for you to let go of the pain, hurt, trauma, or anger.

This does not give you license to vent your feelings on anyone who upsets you. If you were to do this, you could get put away. For instance, if you were stopped by a highway patrolman who gave you a speeding ticket and you vented your anger all over him, you might get an additional ticket or get taken to jail. You want to take care of yourself so that you don't get your vote canceled. Over the years I have found that using a surrogate to release and vent the emotions can be very helpful. In the same way that role-playing helps reenact the situation and allows you to air your feelings, using a friend or surrogate can help you discharge the built-up energy as well.

To have access to your emotions but to also be able to monitor their release is essential to successful emotional management. You need to be able to choose where and when you release your emotions.

4) COMMUNICATE WHATEVER IS NECESSARY

You do not want to confuse communicating with experiencing, expressing, and releasing the emotions. People confuse these four, thinking: If I communicate to the person, then I have released the "charge." Communication is an important step, and it can happen in many ways. You can do it verbally, face to face, over the phone, or in writing. You want to make sure that you release the "charge" on the feeling before you communicate it to the person who has inspired a particular feeling. It is important that you communicate responsibly. After all, you want to produce a result, not just blow people away. It may feel great to release your feelings, especially after so many years of suppressing them, but you need to see the result venting will produce. Often the emotional charge is disproportionate to the stimulus in the situation. This happens as a result of the accumulation of past unexperienced situations. When you don't address the emotional aspect hidden within the message, you are a loaded gun waiting to shoot an unsuspecting person who might accidently hit the trigger. You may offend, insult, and alienate people if you do not separate these two steps.

By dealing with communication as a two-step process, you take care of both people. You, yourself, are taken care of because you attend to your feelings and honor them. The other person is taken care of because you have communicated responsibly, in a respectful way, and in a manner that can be accepted. You want to ensure that you are approachable and rational in your delivery, so that the message is received and not rejected.

5) COMPLETION OF THE CYCLE

At this phase you reflect on the process you have been engaged in to determine what lessons are to be learned from the experience. You look to see what you would do differently next time. In other words, you do not go on to the next situation without taking the time to see how you can grow from this one. To repeat patterns habitually which have not been examined or released is addictive behavior. Ultimately, each experience of intense feeling can be a healing from the past as well as an opportunity for growth in the future.

THE
SECRET LEDGER
OF THE
SUBCONSCIOUS
■

Another manifestation of feelings in daily life is the storing of incomplete feelings. When a feeling has not been experienced, expressed, or released, it lodges itself within your psyche and hovers there until the time when it is called forth to be of service. And it is always called forth to be of service.

Sarita took a phone message from Herb for Ben, and forgot to give it to him. She was embarrassed about it, but didn't say anything. When Herb called later that week, he asked if Sarita had given him the message. Ben dismissed it, but noticed that an important message had been dropped. Later that week, Ben was to meet Sarita for a luncheon meeting with papers which she needed to sign to formalize a contract that would accelerate her commission check. Ben arrived at lunch without the papers. When Sarita asked Ben about the papers, he felt chagrined because he had totally forgotten to bring them.

On the surface these incidents look innocent enough, but upon closer examination and considering their relative proximity in time, there was a definite cause-and-effect relationship between them. Ben ignored his feelings. But Ben's feelings did not forget Sarita. Those feelings needed to be attended to. In truth, Ben felt unimportant and left out. The feelings would get the attention they deserved one way or another. Ben's feelings, even though seemingly unimportant, were logged in his subconscious. Events like this started occurring more frequently, so that eventually Ben and Sarita were hardly speaking. Ben's ignored feelings demanded vindication. Ben and Sarita came in for a consultation to sort out their association and get things back on track. After they had traced the clues that led to the original incident, they were amazed at how important feelings are to every relationship. It shocked them to discover that such a trivial situation could cause a major communication breakdown.

The subconscious works in very mysterious ways; it never forgets anything. The subconscious keeps a record of all interactions, much like a videotape of your life. The subconscious is also the referee who monitors that the game of life is played fairly. The most important information that is documented by the subconscious is data pertaining to your feelings. When your feelings get hurt, it is recorded. When you have felt ignored or abandoned, it is documented. When you let yourself down, the subconscious knows, and it will never let you forget. The subconscious keps a ledger of checks and balances to ensure that all is fair and just.

There is a myth in the world that hurt feelings dissipate

and disappear. The expression "time heals all wounds" represents this myth. The truth of the matter is that the subconscious vindicates all wrongdoings. After recording the scenario, noting the wrongdoings (and rightdoings), the internal device then builds a case amassing information in order to balance the score. So you may say, "It doesn't matter," "I don't care," or "It's no big deal," in order to save face and appear aloof. You may be severing the feelings one more time in order to camouflage your real inner truth. The subconscious knows, and will take care of it in due time. The ignored feelings will demand to be recognized.

FORGOTTEN FEELINGS FEED THE NEGAHOLIC

■

Feelings: Knowing them, getting in touch with them, and managing them so that they work for you is pivotal to the negaholic recovery process. If you are disconnected from your feelings and automatically pursue mood alterators, then you encourage negaholic behavior. Remember, all addictive behavior is motivated by either the pursuit of or the avoidance of a feeling. All addictions are geared to relieving, avoiding, or anesthetizing a feeling. So being aware and monitoring your feelings is fundamental to the recovery process.

Since people infrequently discuss feelings, they are often at a loss as to the labels to assign to what they are feeling. The list on the following page is geared to help you sort out and label what you are feeling.

FEELING WORDS

abandoned	desirous	guilty	niggardly	sorrowful
adequate	despairing	gullible	obnoxious	spiteful
adamant	destructive	happy	obsessed	spoiled
affectionate	determined	hateful	obsolete	startled
agonized	different	heavenly	odd	stingy
alienated	diffident	helpful	outraged	strange
ambivalent	diminished	helpless	overwhelmed	stuffed
angry	discontented	high	pain	stupid
annoyed	disgusted	homesick	panicked	stunned
anxious	distracted	honored	peaceful	stupefied
apathetic	distraught	horrible	persecuted	suffering
astounded	disturbed	hostile	petrified	sure
awed	dominated	hurt	pity	sympathetic
bad	divided	hysterical	pleased	talkative
beautiful	dubious	ignored	pressured	tempted
betrayed	eager	immortal	prim	tenacious
bitter	ecstatic	imposed upon	prissy	tenuous
bitchy	electrified	impressed	proud	tense
blissful	empty	inadequate	quarrelsome	tentative
bold	enchanted	inferior	queer	terrible
brave	energetic	infatuated	rageful	threatened
burdened	enjoyment	infuriated	rapture	tired
bored	envious	inspired	refreshed	thwarted
calm	excited	intimidated	rejected	trapped
capable	evil	isolated	relaxed	troubled
captivated	exasperated	jealous	relieved	ugly
challenged	exhausted	joyous	remorse	uneasy
charmed	exhilarated	jumpy	restless	unloved
cheated	fascinated	kind	reverent	unsettled
cheerful	fearful	lazy	rewarded	used
childish	flustered	lecherous	righteous	violent
clever	foolish	left out	resentful	vehement
combative	frantic	lonely	sad	vital
competitive	frustrated	longing	satisfied	vulnerable
condemned	frightened	loving (love)	scared	vivacious
confused	free	low	servile	voluptuous
conspicuous	full	lustful	settled	warm
contented	furious	mad	sexy	weird
contrite	freaked out	mean	shocked	wicked
cruel	gay	melancholy	sick	wonderful
crushed	glad	miserable	silly	weepy
culpable	good	mystical	skeptical	worried
deceitful	gratified	naughty	sleepy	worthless
defeated	great	nervous	sneaky	zany
delighted	greedy	nutty	solemn	

Once you've found your feelings, then it is time to manage the voices in your head.

FIVE

THE VOICES WITHIN

■

Have you heard voices in your head? No, I'm not asking you to admit that you're crazy, nor am I provoking modern-day Joan of Arcs to stand up and be counted. Just ask yourself if you have heard a chattering in your head, voices that talk to you. See if you can recall a dialogue within your head which was either commenting about you or others. If you have, you're not alone. The vast majoirty of adults experience inner voices.

WHAT ARE THE VOICES

■

The voices can do monologues or dialogues, but most often they simply chatter at you. Some people haven't differentiated between their thoughts, their intuition, their inner "messages" and "the voices." There is a distinct difference between them. If you are going to stop being a negaholic, then you must be able to tell the difference between these communication centers.

Thoughts are ideas and concepts that originate in the left side of the brain and involve deliberation, reflection, consideration, contemplation, reasoning, and speculation. Thoughts usually follow a logical progression.

The voices of the mind are involuntary chatterings which use data from life experiences in a logical, rational, and reasonable manner. They tend to talk *to* you or *at* you. They advise, direct, and guide you in ways which keep you safe.

Intuition is nonintellectual perception without reasoning, in which you experience awareness or knowledge of something without conscious attention.

Inner messages are the direct knowing of information which emanates from within. They are irrational, illogical, and unreasonable. They embody important information and counsel, often referring to a higher order of self.

When people cannot differentiate between these communcation centers, the decision-making process becomes very difficult. In fact, they frequently don't know which set of data to listen to. Between their conscious thoughts, their intuition, their messages, the voices of their minds, and all the advice they receive from family and friends, it is no wonder that they get stuck. Getting stuck translates into feelings of confusion, doubt, uncertainty and/or fear.

Very often the voices have grown strong and loud and will drown out the subtler inner messages. Sometimes people doubt that they even have messages, since the voices of the mind are bassoons of their inner commentary. The voices are most often a composite of parents, teachers, and authority figures who were feeding you data in order to:

- get you to achieve results
- protect you from hurt, failure, or rejection

- promote remorse or guilt so that you atone for wrong-doings so that you will grow into a person with the right set of values.

It is very important to realize at this point that the voices are not bad, but rather well-intentioned, misdirected, clumsy helpers doing the wrong thing at a bad time in the worst way. Like in a Laurel and Hardy movie, good intentions create havoc through lack of training.

The voices in your head can take a variety of different forms, but often they are negative. They have a tendency to criticize, judge, evaluate, invalidate, find fault with, and dwell on the negative.

Let's say, for example, that you are about to embark upon a new venture and this internal voice starts to tell you that "you can't," "you shouldn't," "you'll botch it," "you don't know enough." These inner messages might cause you to have second thoughts, become tentative, talk yourself out of your action plan. If you got far enough into the venture you might be programmed to fail. If you want to deal with these voices effectively, you have to identify and then manage them.

IDENTIFYING INTERNAL VOICES
◼

The process of identifying your internal voice is not terribly complicated, but it does have some very specific and necessary steps. You must be willing to take each step and follow the directions to completion in order to get the results. My clients most often want to be able to quiet the voices, reprogram them, and turn them into allies.

If these are the results that you have targeted for your own well-being, then read on. In order to turn your voices into allies, you must first know what you are dealing with. To do so, follow this four-step process:

1. *Listen* to the voices in your mind, and really hear what they are saying to you.
2. *Write* down what they are saying, or
3. *Talk* the voices out into a tape recorder or dictating machine.
4. *Describe* a visual image you create for the voices. Close your eyes and picture what or who is saying the words to you. Use your imagination and be creative in depicting the creature(s) inside your head.

Children are excellent at using their imaginations to conjure up pictures. They are inventive at naming and interacting with all kinds of creatures emanating from their imaginations. If you can remember back to your own childhood, you will recall that you most probably used your imagination in much the same way. That child of so many years ago, the one with such a vivid imagination, is still lurking inside you. That child is still as fanciful, whimsical, and creative as you were back then. Over the years you have learned very effectively how to be an adult, and in certain respects you may have relegated your child within to a closet deep inside yourself.

THE CHOICE: TRAIN, NEGOTIATE, OR EVICT

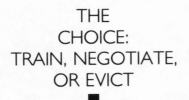

After you have acknowledged the existence of your inner voices and given them an identity, you can either train them, negotiate with them, or evict them from the premises. It is as if a stray dog arrived at your door one cold evening and you didn't have the heart to turn it away. Now, five years later, the dog is still with you; the only problem is that you don't especially like it. Or perhaps a long-lost cousin came to visit you for the holidays and never went home. The question is not whether you like stray dogs or whether your cousin is your favorite person; the question is really whether you have chosen to co-habit with them.

You may very well have strays and miscellaneous relatives dwelling within your head who are unwanted guests. You may have been putting up with them because you're nice and you wouldn't want to inconvenience anyone. You may not want to rock the boat, upset the status quo, or have anyone get angry at you. So you put up with, tolerate, stifle the feelings, and are polite, accommodating, and charming to those unwanted mental house guests. Well, it may be time to clean house. Not that you have to actually evict anyone from your mental domicile. As I said before, you have three options: train, negotiate, or evict.

If the inhabitant is a stray, you may want to consider training him or her. If the inhabitant is your cousin, you may want to consider negotiating so that you have a win-win situation. If all else fails, rather than suffering in silence you may want to consider eviction. You take a good sober look at what will work for you in your life.

You have a choice about who lives in your head and what they say to you. Just because these characters are there does not mean that they are invited, wanted, or permanent residents. They may just be old lodgers, vagrants, strays, relatives, or ghosts from the past who have become permanent fixtures in the enviroment. They became comfortable, and never left. It is time for you to take stock of who is inhabiting your internal domain.

Perhaps one or more of your voices has been running the show and you have been sitting by, like a couch potato watching TV. Or you may feel like a captive, trapped in a lecture from which you can't escape. But you can escape. This is your own head. This is the head that accompanies you everywhere you go, every day of your life. You get to choose if this head is going to chatter at you or if you are going to determine who is in there and what they say to you. You need to remember who is at the helm. Whose place is this anyway?

ELENA,
THE
WORKAHOLIC
■

A client of mine was extremely articulate in verbalizing her internal voices. She was aware of the voices, found it relatively easy to visualize them, and was willing to discuss them openly with me. Her mental images, as well as her descriptions of the roles these characters play, were so graphic that I felt it would be helpful to study her process.

LISTENING

Elena, a particularly successful workaholic, was driving herself crazy.

As she explained, "I know that my situation is self-imposed, but I am trapped in my own patterns. In other words, I know I am doing all of this to myself, but I don't know how to undo it!"

We got down to the specifics, and she told me that she had approximately two free hours for herself per week. Her life was filled with teaching, preparation for her classes, clients, writing, family, and research. She had no free time and was feeling squeezed and claustrophobic. I asked her if she wanted to tackle the form, by which I meant time management and schedules, or the substance, of her internal patterns, which continually re-created the same situations. She replied that she wanted to look within herself. She felt that if we focused on time management, she would only repeat the same old patterns and overload her life once again. She said that she wanted to get beyond the symptom and look at the core of the problem.

I asked her to tell me what the interior voices were saying. She said there was a voice that was driving her all the time. The voice was relentless about getting things done, so much so that she had to justify her existence on the planet. Each day she had to accomplish enough tasks to prove that she had a

right to be here and was in fact a worthwhile person. The
problem was the absence of a gauge. She would never know
when she had accomplished enough to satisfy the inner voice.
There was no *there* to get to. I asked her if she could put a
name on the voice. She called the voice Laurel. I asked her to
describe Laurel to me.

DESCRIBING
She said, "Laurel is perfect. She always does everything right.
Her hair is pulled back in a bun, she wears high collars, and
longer-than-average skirts. She wears little makeup or jewelry,
and horn-rimmed glasses on her nose. She is righteous and
better than everyone else. Laurel is named Laurel because she
receives all the laurel wreaths. Laurel gets more done than
anyone else in the world, and she prides herself on that. She
does not tolerate laziness, indecision, or excuses. She is ruthless
in her management of herself. She runs the show with an iron
hand, and always meets her deadlines."

I asked Elena how she felt with Laurel at the helm.

"Whipped, beaten, driven, and frantic inside."

I then asked, "Is Laurel the only voice you are aware of?"

"No, there is a playful voice, too, which likes to have fun."

I asked for more information on this other voice.

She said, "This voice wants to go dancing, go to the beach,
go for coffee, hang out, and play. She is scantily dressed, and
likes to change clothes with her mood. Sometimes she is in
shorts and a tank top, other times she dons a red, skintight,
fringed dress; other times she will prance about in a negligée.
This voice likes to be frivolous, spend money, have a good time,
and go shopping."

"Is that all?"

"No! This voice likes to wear sexy clothes and flirt with
men. This voice wants to laugh, and sing, and make love all
night long with no thought of tomorrow. This is the voice that
could really get me into trouble. Both Laurel and I are afraid
of this voice."

I asked her what she could call this voice.

"Without hesitation she replied, "Rosie!"

"How do Laurel and Rosie get along?"

Elena said, "Laurel has to keep Rosie out of sight and under wraps. Rosie is an embarrassment to Laurel. Laurel has spent a lot of time building a reputation, establishing credibility, and building a track record. If Rosie came out of the closet she would ruin everything for Laurel. So Laurel is compelled to keep Rosie silenced and out of sight."

I asked if these were the only two voices she was aware of.

"No, there is a sad, maudlin, pathetic, helpless, depressed, lonely woman lurking within. She wears a faded housedress, with hose that have enormous runs and bag down around her ankles. Her hair is mousy gray-brown and in need of attention. Her nails are broken and ragged, and she gazes downward. Her breasts droop to her waist and her stomach extends to reach them. She is lifeless, and has no motivation to be or do anything. She has been beaten down by the rejections, the losses, the tarnished dreams, and the profound pain of failure."

Again I asked her the name of the voice.

"Helen," she replied.

I asked how Helen interacted with Laurel and Rosie.

She said, "Wait, there is one more!"

I asked for clarification.

She said, "There is a hit man who works for Laurel. He is in charge of enforcing martial law when Rosie has taken charge and is running the show. This man has an arsenal which is capable of destroying everything."

I asked his name.

She said solemnly, "Mehetibel." She added, "It works like this: Laurel does a great job eighty-five to ninety percent of the time, but sooner or later Rosie sneaks (or slinks) to the foreground and takes over the show. Laurel gets very upset but is incapable of controlling Rosie once she is out of the closet. Laurel then calls in Mehetibel and orders him to clean house. Mehetibel desecrates everything in sight, including Laurel, and all that is left is Helen. Hopeless, useless, and beaten Helen. Helen, who doesn't possess the will to do anything, stands alone. After Helen has had the opportunity to be in the foreground for enough time, gradually Laurel is resurrected and begins to run the show all over again. This is the scenario which repeats itself over and over again. I can't take it anymore, and what's more I don't want to."

I asked her what she wanted.

She said that unless she integrated Laurel and Rosie into herself she would keep repeating the pattern over and over again.

I asked what she wanted to do with Mehetibel and Helen.

"Once Laurel and Rosie are integrated, I want them to leave." We embarked upon the quest to integrate the internal voices of Laurel and Rosie.

WHERE
DO THE
VOICES
COME FROM
■

The voices, which were developed from two sources, are aspects of Elena's personality. Significant people in her childhood imprinted their personalities and words on her to such a degree that their influence formed an identity which became an aspect of her personality. This is not a subpersonality of Elena's, but rather a feature which has emerged as a full-blown inner voice.

Whenever there is inner dialogue between different characters, there is a schism within. When you're at one with yourself, there is no need for a conversation. It is when you become at odds with yourself that there is a need for interaction. Usually the split emerges out of conflict. The discussion or debate is engaged because of unreconciled discrepancies which exist in your identity. When the self is out of alignment, the discord is the reflection of the lack of integration between the various imprints you received from primary role models in childhood.

The inner dialogue between the different characters drowns out the subtle inner messages which come forth from the self. In order to hear the messages, you need to integrate the characters so that they are quiet and you can once again listen.

The process of integration occurs through talking, visualizing, dramatizing, ritualizing, and experiencing the unresolved conflicts from the past.

Visualization is seeing with the mind's eye what you want to become reality. It involves using your imagination and creativity to conjure up the picture you want to manifest. You close your eyes and fantasize the ideal situation which you desire, in order to regroove the brain, see the image, feel the feelings, and hear the words associated with it. If you can involve as many senses as possible, you can bring texture, depth, and realness to your image. This will enable the image to take on a life of its own and and the involvement of the senses will merge the gap between fantasy and reality.

INTERNAL
VOICE
MANAGEMENT
■

As long as there is a schism between two different internal characters, then you are at odds with yourself. There is an internal battle raging, the battleground of which is your mind.

NEGOTIATION
■

The schism needs to be resolved so that the different characters are aligned rather than antagonistic. This process of resolution is called "integration." Integrating the internal characters is similar to the mediation process between people. The characters are dealt with as separate. Each one has its own agenda, set of values, and style.

If you choose to keep all of your characters within you, then you need to teach them how to live together in harmony. You must negotiate with them. They need to become a team that is rooting for you and helping you to get what you want. This means that you become the coach of the team and start calling the plays, and have your inner voices work together as a unit. It doesn't matter that the players are different; good teams always have diversity. What matters is that they can transcend their differences and work together for your good. You must orchestrate the different parts into harmony, and not just stand by watching the show, feeling victimized by the various characters who are in charge.

Getting acquainted with the voices is a beneficial process. It is a journey within the interior of your mind to meet your internal players, your cast. You may have one internal voice, or two, or several. It is not significant how many internal voices you have; what is important is that you discover who is in there and what they are saying to you. Then and only then can you choose what you want to do about them.

If you do not make a choice about who is inside, or train, negotiate, or evict those internal characters, you will feel victimized by the voices which have taken over your internal territory. The internal voices may personify real people from your past or they may be a composite of several people. In fact, your inner voices may be creatures, animals, or monsters which your imagination has generated. Jenna's situation was exactly that.

JENNA
AND THE
HAIRY MONSTER
■

A client named Jenna came to me in tears one day saying, "I'm so hard on myself, and I can't stop it!"

I asked what was happening.

"I can never do anything right; no matter what I do I can never do it right!"

We went through a process similar to Elena's. I asked for a description of the voice, and she told me of the brutal, abusive, and vicious comments this voice would make to her. I then asked for a description.

She said, "He is big and hairy and stands about seven feet tall. He carries a huge club and every time I say or do anything that he doesn't like, he hits me with the club. I've been hit so many times that I'm bruised and bloody. I think it is actually affecting my posture, I'm starting to walk hunched over."

"What is the name of the voice?"

She replied, "Thor."

I asked what she wanted to do about Thor.

"I want to domesticate him. He is strong and powerful, so I don't want to get rid of him, but I would like him on my team. I need to teach him manners, and how to talk to me." She added, almost as an afterthought, "I need to get rid of that damn club!"

We set out to domesticate Thor.

Thor is not inherently bad or good, he has just gotten out of hand. It is like having a Great Pyrenees dog who has taken over the entire house. He is not yet paper trained, and he is in the process of ruining all the carpets in the house, as well as knocking over miscellaneous pieces of furniture. Your house is in disarray because you have relinquished control and the animal who has taken over has different priorities. Your house, in this instance, is your mind. If you have some creature who has taken over your "house" and is running roughshod over you, then it is time to grab hold of the reins.

The solution is not necessarily to evict Thor, although that, of course, is an option. The strategy is to evaluate whether or not Thor is helpful to you, and worth taking the time to train to bring on board as an ally. In this case, Jenna wanted to keep Thor around. She felt that he had some real possibilities. She opted to train him, to domesticate the beast, as the best possible solution.

If Thor were indeed a Great Pyrenees dog, you would then have the best of both worlds: a wonderful dog and a beautiful home.

In order to manage your internal voices effectively, you need to suspend judgment while dealing with them. As you have seen with Jenna, the voices are not always people from your past; they may be a composite of personalities which your mind has woven together to form a whole new entity. In certain instances, the internal voices may not be people at all, they may all be animals, as in the case with Sylvia.

SYLVIA
AND
THE DOGS
∎

One day Sylvia, a new client, came to see me. She had been very successful in the past, but she was now in a funk and wanted to change her situation. She complained that despite the fact that she had written six books, had her own TV show, and had lived all over the world, there were times when she felt totally powerless. We embarked upon the same journey to meet and become acquainted with her inner voices.

I asked when she had these feelings, and she spoke about times when she felt insecure and desperately needed approval.

"What do the voices say to you?"

She responded, "They say: Please like me, I want to play too, let me come along."

I asked her for a description of the creature attached to the voice.

"It's a little wet cocker spaniel with its tongue hanging out, and its tail wagging, jumping up and gently scratching with its paws."

"What is its name?"

She replied contemptuously, "Cocker."

When I inquired why she appeared angry, she said, "I hate cocker spaniels, they require so much attention."

I asked when Cocker appeared.

"When I am confused, insecure, feeling inadequate, feeling lonely, needing attention, and longing for validation." She added, "I hate the thought of me being like a cocker spaniel!"

I asked if there was another voice within or if this was the only one.

She said, "No, there's definitely more than one. There is my powerful, knowing, confident, capable voice, the voice that has gotten me everything I have ever wanted."

I asked what this voice looked like, and was told that it was "sleek, strong, and shiny; a champion, a veritable force to be reckoned with."

I asked about the size and shape of this creature and was informed with an enormous amount of certainty that this voice belonged to a Doberman pinscher. He was named, appropriately, Dobie.

For whatever reason, all of Sylvia's internal voices were cast as dogs. She had a regular kennel within. She needed to decide if she wanted to keep every single dog or to let some of them go. After she had chosen the dogs, she then had to see what role each would play in her life. She had to assign each a specific function, give it the words she wanted it to say to her, and ensure it delivered its lines on cue. It is O.K. to have a kennel within as long as you are running the kennel, and it serves your purposes. Don't hand over the control of your life to the dogs!

Even if you have done so, however, all is not lost. You simply need to take charge of the situation.

INTERNAL CASTING AND SCRIPTING
■

While we are talking about ensuring that those inner voices deliver their lines properly, we should pursue another line of attack in dealing with internal voice management. This is internal casting and scripting. I don't know if you have ever had the feeling that your life was a movie, but Sonia often did. She frequently wondered if Alan Funt wasn't hiding behind some tree, poised and ready to capture it all on his inimitable *Candid Camera* for the amusement of future generations. At these times, she would take a step back and ask herself, "What part am I playing?" Sometimes it would seem as if she were the leading lady of this entertaining film. Then there were other times when she would glance at herself and observe that she was playing the damsel in distress, or, perhaps, the tragic heroine. One day she was the busy executive; the next she became a femme fatale. The worst times were when she viewed herself as an extra in her own movie. It would seem as if she had lost touch with the story line, the plot, and the production. It was as if all the action was happening around her, and her own role was superfluous.

You are ultimately the director, writer, producer, and star of your own movie. Sometimes, you may forget this!

Ask yourself, "Who is in my movie? What part(s) am I playing?" Are you the young ingénue, the middle-aged character actor, the supporting actor, the leading male or female? Are you the villain, the hero, the damsel in distress, or the "bit-player," the cameo, or the walk-on? Do your parts change? If so, how often? Do you like the parts you are playing? If not, would you like to change them? If yes, what are the ideal parts you *would* like to be playing?

In order to make any changes in the way you relate to yourself, you must first come to terms with who is inside of you. As the producer, scriptwriter, set designer, casting agent, and lead in your movie, you are the one, and the only one, who gets to call the shots in your life. You also, and most importantly, get to determine what kind of a character the leading woman or man is. Until you are aware of who is inside, you cannot write the script or cast the film. You need to unravel the internal dialogues to see who is doing the talking and what they are saying. Once you are aware of what is being said, then you can choose:

- if you want these characters in the movie at all
- if you want them to speak or not

- what you want them to say
- how you want them to deliver their lines

THE
DISOWNED
SELVES
■

These internal voices are like disowned selves who are vying for attention. They are often the parts of you which you have either abandoned, abdicated, ignored, or idolized. Creating drama in your life is often a desperate way of trying to be seen by others when you can't find yourself any other way. At any rate, they are separate from the essential you and need to be integrated.

Neila had a disowned self named Sheila. Sheila was her shy, timid withdrawn side, who acted as if she had been beaten and badly abused as a child. Neila, the real person, could not remember much of her childhood, and would react in an impatient, critical manner whenever Sheila would surface. Sheila wanted to be comforted and held. She desperately needed to feel loved. She was so withdrawn and insecure that she was not in touch with what she wanted, nor could she verbalize it in order to get it. Her behavior was whiny and clutchy, which would drive Neila crazy. Through discussion, Neila discovered Sheila, this disowned part of herself, and found a way to cast and script into her life so that she stopped being repulsive and became lovable.

The new approach that Neila devised was listening to Sheila with empathy, trying to understand her fears and insecurities. Neila would tell Sheila that whatever she was feeling was O.K., and that she still loved her. When Sheila would emit the message that she wanted to be held, Neila would either take the time to sit quietly holding and rocking herself, saying, "I care about you; your feelings matter to me." Neila would then give Sheila words to say: "I care about you also. I am just scared and insecure. Please don't abandon me, but love me. Help me to be strong; I am willing to learn; I am just very fearful. Please be patient with me." In this way, your essential self can have a dialogue with one of your disowned characters and begin teamwork. The steps go like this:

- find out who the disowned self is
- begin a dialogue with this self
- help each side to work together as a team
- help each one to merge into a peaceful union
- begin to love all the parts of you

The negaholic is victimized either consciously or unconsciously by the voices within. You need to understand the mechanism which forms the voices, to see how they are nourished and what you need to do to take control of them so that you are operating from a place of choice regarding your life.

Since negaholism is an addiction, you need to have an active daily program as an antidote to the self-negation which the voices may have been inflicting on you for many years. No addiction simply goes away with awareness. Remember that you are hooked! You have become an addict to self-negation, and self-sabotage! Until you admit that you are a negaholic, you will merely be playing with the ideas presented in this book. The next chapter will give you tried-and-true techniques to help you stop punishing yourself.

SIX

BE
ON THE
ALERT FOR

■

The large majority of people do not spend every waking moment beating themselves up, but when you least expect it a negattack will sneak up on you, jump you from behind and before you know it, you will have a full-blown attack taking over the driver's seat of your life. If you come from a dysfunctional home, you probably automatically think in terms of problem/solution, pain/killer, not O.K./fix it. You think in terms of finding instant panaceas which make everything all right immediately. You probably have very little patience or trust that things will ever change or be different.

You therefore need to understand the anatomy of self-negation, how the negativity works, and what brings on the negattack, so that you can detect the warning signs before you have totally gone down the tubes.

THE
ANATOMY
OF SELF-TORMENT
■

Self-torment can start with an incident, a thought, a feeling or a combination of the above. The incident could be any situation in which you do not live up to your expectations of yourself. If you expect that you are supposed to do everything perfectly, then whenever you do not perform up to your standard of perfection you've left yourself wide open for a negattack. You could go for a bike ride, fall off and beat yourself for hurting yourself. You could go to a party and have a terrible time and beat yourself for not staying home. You could go grocery shopping, and forget to buy something and beat yourself for not getting everything that you needed. You could lie out in the sun and find fault with yourself for getting burned. You could criticize yourself for not making phone calls, for not writing a letter, for forgetting a friend's birthday, for letting something burn in the oven. There are limitless opportunities to be hard on yourself. All of these opportunities for harshness are situation-driven.

Some of the thoughts that could engage the self-flagellation mechanism are: "I never should have . . . ," or "If only I'd . . . ," or "I really blew it when I . . . ." These thoughts look back regretfully at the past (maybe just a past moment) and underscore the events that weren't as you would have liked. Not only did situations not work out as you would have wished, but you are being personally blamed for the way your life is now. The thoughts usually kick in after an incident has occurred. Sometimes you can be carrying punishment within you years after incidents happened. For instance, "I never should have married her," or "I never should have sold that stock," or "I never should have left that job." You can look back remorsefully and regretfully at almost anything and dredge up enough evidence to knock yourself around. You can also get creative and look ahead, anticipating how awful something is going to be: "You'll probably blow that audition," or "You'll probably screw things up with this relationship as well as all the rest," or "You know what a klutz you are, you won't be able to ski, don't even bother trying."

On the other hand, the cruelty could start with a feeling. You could wake up with low energy, a subtle malaise, or a low-grade depression. You could just feel physically bad, and be mean to yourself for not feeling terrific. You could feel down as a result of an interaction with a friend, a merchant, or the driver of another car. For instance, you could have stayed up late dancing and drinking and wake up the next morning with a terrible hangover and start berating yourself for going out the night before.

Or you could overeat at lunch, feel stuffed and be bad to yourself for overeating. You could talk with a friend who told you that you hurt her feelings and then seize the opportunity to use these feelings against yourself. After your banker tells you that you can't get the loan you applied for, you nag at yourself for not being rich, for spending your money unwisely, or for not having inherited wealth. After having pulled out of a side street without looking and almost hit an oncoming car you seize the chance to lambaste yourself for having your thoughts elsewhere. Or you may feel anxious about an upcoming exam and you hold yourself in contempt for not studying earlier, longer, or harder.

In addition to whatever you are feeling or avoiding feeling, there is also the rush associated with the psychological mania. The intensity experienced is the physical, chemical reaction that you have when you mentally flog yourself. Even though the negativity does not feel good, the rush does.

The next thing that happens is that you probably will want to feel better, since you are aggressively inflicting pain on yourself. The desire to feel better may be translated into pleasure, the avoidance of pain, the desire to feel numb, to feel stimulated or euphoric. The average person would do something to get out of this condition. This may be a conscious or an unconscious decision. The action may be impulsive or premeditated, but usually there is a drive to change your circumstances. You may then decide to indulge yourself in an activity, a behavior, a process, or a substance which can and does change your mood. You may go for a walk, watch TV, smoke a cigarette, have a drink, have something with sugar in it, or take a drug ranging from aspirin to marijuana, from Valium to cocaine. You find that the activity, the process, or the substance has done the job. Your mood is altered, you feel different and perhaps better, at least temporarily. You may feel numb, or pleasured, or calm, or high, or euphoric, but the bottom line is that your mood or condition is different from what it was before. For a while things are O.K.

Eventually the mood alterator wears off, and feelings similar to the ones you were experiencing before you indulged yourself and altered your mood will probably start to return. You can then criticize yourself for altering your mood in the first place. This phase is a "downer." Coupled with abusing yourself for how you are and where you are, you are probably plummeting into a downward spiral. At this point, you may want to reach for the next mood alterator. This new mood alterator may be the same as the last one or it may be different, but since now you are even lower than you were before, there is a need for something to change your state of being significantly.

This is a vicious cycle. You hurt yourself for how you are, what you've done, or what you might do. You feel bad, you want to change the feeling. You do something to change the feeling, and then you fault yourself for doing so. Every time you attack yourself, you get a rush that lets you feel good about feeling bad. You are caught, and you can't win for losing.

Since negaholism is subtle and insidious, it is crucial that you are savvy about the subtle and clandestine ways in which it can creep into your life. You need to be tuned in so that it doesn't get you when you least expect it. You need to be on the lookout for all the different forms of negaholism in case one silently sneaks into your world.

A
SNEAK
ATTACK
FROM BEHIND

You are walking along in a perfectly good mood, having a lovely time, minding your own business, enjoying yourself, and *wham!* it gets you from behind. Out of the blue, with no warning whatsoever, you start having a sneak negattack. It might be stored-up ammunition from the past or momentary insecurities that jump out at you, but jump they did.

In the *Pink Panther* movies, starring Peter Sellers, an Oriental houseboy named Kato would lie in waiting for Inspector Clouseau. Every time Clouseau came in the door, there would always be some sort of sneak attack from Kato, the karate-mad houseboy. With some of us, Kato's behavior can be likened to a mind lying in wait for the proper moment to spring a surprise ambush. You may be most susceptible to ambush in the early morning, before you wake up. The sun may be shining, the birds chirping, and bombs are being dropped on your head before you are even fully awake.

IN
SEARCH OF
UPSETS, PROBLEMS,
AND WORRIES

If everything seems to be working, then you unconsciously start rooting around for something to get upset about. You possess an internal Geiger counter which attracts problems, and if it is not functioning then you go in hot pursuit of something to worry about.

While talking to Erma, Sadie said, "I think my heating bill got sent to the wrong address."

Erma responded, "So, don't worry about it, they'll find out and send it to you."

Sadie countered, "But what if they turn off my heat? I'll freeze!"

Erma replied, "Don't be silly, you're not going to freeze to death, just call them in the morning and tell them that you think that the bill went to the wrong address, and have it corrected."

Sadie persisted, "Everything is on computers now. When I call, a computer answers the phone. Nobody knows what is going on. I'll never get this straightened out."

"Of course you will," Emma argued. "It's a simple matter, and you'll get it straightened out with no problem. Stop worrying."

Sadie contended, "But what if it's too late, and they have already started to shut off the heat? I could die by tomorrow night!"

Erma looked Sadie straight in the eyes and said, "Are you looking for something to get upset about? If you are, this is as good as anything, but I really don't think there is any reason to get alarmed."

How often do you find yourself taking inventory on current problems? This is not strange behavior, by the way. If you are a compulsive, addicted personality, you will (on some level) enjoy the rush of being worried, upset, or concerned about something. The drama is, in fact, preferable to everything working smoothly. Watch for telltale signs when you are looking for things to get upset about.

LIFE'S GETTING TOO GOOD, LET'S SCREW IT UP

This one is subtle. Things start really going your way. You have just gotten your ideal job, and a raise as well, and you

can't believe it; it's a dream come true. On top of that, a dear
friend calls to say that she is going away for an extended period
of time, and asks if you would mind house-sitting for her in
her beautiful home. And you have a date with the person you've
wanted to date for over a year. You feel joyous about your life,
your friends, and all that is happening. Do you start to worry
and fret about what could go wrong? Do you start doubting
your reality, feeling that everything is going just *too* well? Do
you start acting suspicious, waiting for the other shoe to drop?
Do you question the validity of what is happening? Do you
question whose life you're living, since it doesn't resemble
yours? Do you find yourself saying things like, "Just wait, I'll
get transferred to Siberia," or "The apartment will probably
be burglarized while I'm staying there"? Do you start doing
silly, subtle, and stupid things to undermine your successes?
Do you have a difficult time accepting that your life really *could*
be wonderful, happy, and everything you've ever wanted? Do
you have preconceived limits about how good your life can get?

WOE IS ME,
WHAT CAN
THE MATTER BE?

You don't know what is the matter with you. You're not sick,
and everything seems to be going fine. You really have nothing
to complain about, but you just feel off. You have the blahs,
and you're not sure whether to call your doctor, your shrink,
your hairdresser, or go to the beach.

The blahs are often the beginning. Watch out for them!
Before you start to psychoanalyze yourself, and then beat yourself for not being how you should be (perfect), try another approach. See if you can give yourself permission to be just exactly
how you are. Let yourself know that it's O.K. to not be terrific,
or sparkly, or on top of the world. Consider letting yourself be
just exactly the way you are, without fixing, changing, rear-
ranging, or analyzing. You may be in for a surprise.

HELP!
I CAN'T
FIND MY
FEELINGS
■

Since most of us have been out of touch with our feelings for so long, it isn't surprising that from time to time you may not have a clue as to what you are actually feeling. This is quite normal. When you are not certain about what you are feeling, don't jump on your case and attack yourself for not knowing. Be gentle and give yourself permission to feel whatever you are feeling with compassion.

Go through the list of feeling words, and see if one jumps out at you. If one resonates, write it down, and say the words to yourself out loud. See if you can activate the feeling from within. If the word alone doesn't act as a sufficient catalyst to bring up the feeling, try doing something physical to activate your cardiovascular system. Get your heart pumping, and work yourself into an out-of-breath condition, then read the list of words again, and see if you can feel. If you still can't, then read a sad book, any animal story from childhood, or go to a sad movie.

THE
FEAR
TAKEOVER
■

Sally has just decided to marry Brad. She is excited and happy, she is picturing all the wonderful moments, walking hand in hand through grassy fields covered with daisies. She envisions sitting hearthside with a glowing fire and soft romantic music playing in the background, the smell of bread baking in the oven. As she leaves her fantasy, she goes out to get the mail and sees a notice from a collection agency for Brad. She panics.

Her mind takes the ball and runs down the field. What if

he is in bad financial straits? What if he has misrepresented himself and isn't what he says he is? What if he is a gold digger? What if he only wants to marry me for my money? What if he has been an angel throughout our courtship and he is going to turn into a monster after we're married? What if he is really a slob, who sits around the house eating potato chips and drinking beer, and he never helps out, and he expects to be waited on, and I'm going to be trapped? Oh my God, what if this is the worst mistake I've ever made in my life? What am I going to do?

This is called the "Fear Takeover," and it can happen whenever the slightest encouragement is given to any existing doubt.

THE "YEAH-BUTS" ON THE HEELS OF CHOICE

Emily was really excited about her trip to Europe. She was imagining how much fun she would have, and couldn't wait to go. During a conversation with her mother-in-law, she started to get worried. Dorothea was talking about the hostages, and how dangerous the situation was in Europe. She was saying that we were on the verge of war, and it could break out any day.

Emily panicked; right on the heels of her decision to go came the "yeah-buts" urged on by Dorothea.

"Yeah-but" we may be taken hostage!

"Yeah-but" we may never see our families again!

"Yeah-but" we may get killed!

The "yeah-buts" had taken over, had ruined her visions of magical episodes and tripping through castles eating croissants and drinking *café au lait*. She took a nose dive and rapidly started to plummet all the way down.

The "yeah-buts" are little creatures in the mind who resemble Pac-Men. "Yeah-buts" lock on to the worst possible situation and rub your nose in it. Whenever you make a choice, the first step is a rush of excitement, then the dreaminess of imagining the fantasy follows, and then comes a startling dose of reality. When this hits, the "yeah-buts" are in full swing.

I CAN'T
TALK TO
ANYONE, I'M
TOO EMBARRASSED
■

"I don't want to see anyone. I am in such terrible shape and I don't want anyone to know. I wish I could crawl in a hole and die," Lily said, slumping in her chair. She thought she was such bad company that she couldn't be around anyone. Lily had a terrible day, and she was feeling depressed. She hated her job, her boss, and the commute. The negaliens have taken over to such a degree that she doesn't know that they are sitting on her face. She is totally unaware that she has to look around them in order to see. She felt so bad about her life that she would hardly allow any pleasure in, she was wearing sackcloth and ashes psychologically speaking. She was so far gone that she didn't want any human contact. She was too embarrassed to reach out. She was too ashamed for anyone to see her in this condition.

TOSS ME
A LIFE
PRESERVER,
I'M GOING UNDER!
■

This is a state to watch out for. When you are sinking, you need to call for help. This enables someone on dry land to throw you a life preserver and tow you ashore. If you don't call out, no one may know that you need a helping hand, and you may be overlooked on account of your silence. Reaching out to a family member, a friend, or a therapist is critical to your well-being. Swallow your pride and reach out, regardless of your condition. Good friends are there not just when you are in good shape; they are there when you are down, sick, and in need of them.

The next chapter will give you techniques and tools that are proven effective to ward off negaholism. This is your own personal tool kit, full of antidotes to negaholism.

SEVEN

THE
ANTIDOTES
TO THE
BEAT-UP
SYNDROME

■

Ending self-cruelty is a long, slow process that needs daily maintenance, probably for the rest of your life. It is a one-day-at-a-time approach to mental health, emotional well-being, and a happy, stable, productive life. There are several techniques and tools that you must actively use every day in order for the antidote to work. Each tool is designed to establish, develop, or solidify this essential relationship with yourself. All of the tools listed in this book work. They have worked for thousands of people across the United States for more than fifteen years, and they can and will work for you too. But in order for them to work, you must do them. Don't prejudge them; don't evaluate them as too simplistic for you. They are simple, easy, and almost too rudimentary to imagine that they can and do work. Try each one and give them all a chance. After all, the internal beat-up syndrome isn't all that sophisticated, is it?

What is most important is your attitude and determination to break old patterns and transcend your behavior. Don't take these techniques on faith; try them on like pieces of clothing. If you like how they look and feel, then wear them more often. If you don't like them, then take them off. Experiment!

BELIEVING
IN
YOURSELF
■

You need to believe that you can overcome this addiction to negativity, and that you will. You must give yourself permission to be "imperfect" and to understand that from time to time you will backslide. You must reach out for support when you slide, knowing that you are fighting a behavior battle which you learned a long time ago, which has been reinforced for many years and has become habitual. You cannot overcome ingrained habits overnight, nor is it fair to expect that from yourself.

ONE
ACKNOWLEDGMENT
A DAY . . .
■

At the end of the day, take a piece of paper and write down a minimum of ten accomplishments for that day. Make certain to let yourself know that you are pleased with yourself for your ability to get things done.

- List all the "big" items, then the medium-sized items, and don't forget the small ones. If you had a day when you think you didn't get much accomplished, dwell on what you did get done, and notice the small things.
- Shine the spotlight on *what you did do*, not on what you didn't do. Even if you did very little, look for the little

things. You may need to start with brushing your teeth, combing your hair, or taking a shower.
- Search for even the least significant task to acknowledge yourself for. Then do it!

The slogan goes: "Ten acknowledgments a day keep the beat-ups away."

GOOD NEWS/BAD NEWS LIST

■

This is a first cousin to the acknowledgment list. It helps to put things into perspective. Making a list of things you can be pleased about and things that you can be worried or upset about helps to get the balance back. Very often, when you are about to go down the tubes, you can forget that everything is not dismal and hopeless. When your mind gets fixated on the negative, then make yourself a balance sheet and try to see things a little more clearly.

PATS ON THE CHEEK

■

In the morning, after you have gone into the bathroom:

- Look in the mirror for thirty seconds. Don't look "at" yourself. Don't criticize yourself. Don't scrutinize your skin, your hair, your eyebrows, or gums.
- Just be with yourself, by looking into your eyes.
- Feel whatever you feel.
- Notice what those feelings are.
- At the end of thirty seconds say, "Hi, honey (or sweetie), it's going to be all right. I'm here with you and I will

never leave you. You can count on me. You are important to me. We're in this together." You can say any combination of the above. Even if all you say is, "Hi, honey," that is a good start. You can gradually add phrases that make you feel comfortable. The important thing is to take the thirty seconds to connect with yourself. Do this in the morning and in the evening, the last thing before going to bed. If you tend to forget, put a note on the bathroom mirror.

MANAGING
DAILY
STRESS
■

Self-concept is at the crux of stress-related conditions. Balance means feeling in charge, up to the challenge, competent to handle the tasks at hand. When you feel balanced, you know that you have the skills, ability, and motivation to do what is required. When you feel this sense of confidence and competence, it reinforces your sense of self, or your self-esteem.

Conversely, when you feel unable, inadequate, or ill-equipped to meet the immediate challenges, then you feel less confident and capable. Your self-esteem takes a beating. When you feel unable or inadequate, it taxes you and puts a lot of stress on your system.

Stress = out of balance = the organism in trauma; feeling out of control, unable to meet the challenges or the tasks at hand.

The development, promotion, and reinforcement of self-esteem is an important aspect of stress management and totally antithetical to high stress states. Stress sneaks up on you when you least expect it. You become so immersed in whatever problem you are tackling at the moment that you completely lose sight of yourself, your needs, and your well-being. When this happens, it's as if stress has "slimed" you. All of a sudden, it's everywhere, and you never saw it coming.

It takes some attention, as well as heightened awareness, to catch stress before it catches you. To do this, get to know your stress indicators—they are your smoke detectors, that will help you to avert a fire. There are three checkpoints from which to monitor stress. First, the most desirable, is to detect stress from a preventative standpoint, anticipating it before it takes hold. Second, if you missed it before the fact, then you have the option of catching it midstream. By catching it midstream, you can cut the attack off at the pass. If you have been afflicted by stress and its devastating effects, then you have no recourse but to deal with its effects. You can go see your doctor, a stress-management specialist, or simply indulge in mood alterators.

It is important to recognize the early-warning signals which indicate that stress is a concern. Before stress is induced, get to know the warning signs—the lights on your dashboard. What signals indicate that stress is anticipated? Do your shoulders get tight, do you bite your nails, do you get headaches, do you smoke more, do you get an acid stomach, or does your jaw ache from tension? Do you have sleepless nights, or do your eating habits get affected—either by overeating, eating sporadically, or not eating at all. Sure signs of stress anticipation: changes in sleeping, eating, or sexual habits. Other signs of stress are irritability, anxiety, or short-temperedness.

Here are some hot tips about stress, how to notice it, how to manage it, and what to do when it has become a problem. Check over this list and identify your early stress signs.

pain in the neck	tapping feet, finger, pencils
headache	tightness in chest
dry mouth	clenched jaw
shortness of breath	rapid heartbeat
tight shoulders	dizziness
lower back pain	cold or clammy hands
holding your breath	appetite change
irritability, temper loss	shallow breathing
fatigue	sleeplessness

excessive use of stimulants, depressants, or escape mechanisms

If you can detect stress early on, then you can nip it in the bud. What are your symptoms?

SELF-QUESTIONING
TO
GET TO
THE SOURCE

Stop whatever you are doing and take a minute for yourself. At this point, self-inventory is timely and appropriate. You may have become so caught up in your life that you have forgotten to check in with yourself. In order to assess what is going on inside you, you can ask yourself these four simple questions to get to the heart of the matter.

- What am I feeling?
- What do I want?
- What will it take for me to feel back in charge of my life?
- What do I need to do to take care of myself?

If stress sneaks up and seizes hold of you, then you might want to consider stress-reducing devices:

- meditation
- deep breathing after stopping everything
- progressive relaxation
- tension/relaxation
- listening to a tape
- energy release
- speaking up for yourself
- communicating your feelings
- stating your wants

After stress relief, you have a whole new opportunity to assess your lifestyle:

- When do I experience the most stress?
- In which situations do I feel the most stress?
- With whom?
- Where?

Consider what you can do to avoid stress in the future. Ask yourself, "Am I willing to take control of those situations in my life which cause me stress? Am I willing to change my attitude? Do I want to change my response to the stimulus? Am I willing to change a recurring theme which reinforces and self-perpetuates itself? What changes am I *able/willing* to make?"

If you are *not* willing or able to make any lifestyle changes, then you must deal with the signals, or work with the tools to manage stress.

When stress has gotten the best of you, then your self-esteem softens. Why?

- You are the pawn in life—victimized by your circumstances
- You appear to have little or no control
- You feel powerless to effect a result
- You are in a reactive mode—bouncing off the pinball game of life

Self-esteem is developed and reinforced under the following conditions:

- when you know clearly what you want
- when through your own efforts you cause your desired results to happen
- when you initiate or take action based on your own intrinsic motives, desires, intentions

- when you overcome obstacles and challenges and make the seemingly impossible happen
- when you live up to the standards and expectations you have set for yourself

Stress, generally speaking, is essential to the functioning of the organism, but too much stress will tax the organism and render it ineffective. When you experience too much stress, you are in pain, be it emotional, psychological, or physical. When you experience enough pain, you desire relief. Relief often comes in the form of a mood alterator. The thought might be, "I just want to feel better," or "I wish the pain would go away," or "I need a . . ." Stress is the key to the addictive behaviors. When something stressful happens, it activates the neurotransmitters in your brain. If too many neurotransmitters are activated, you become overstimulated and feel pushed over the edge. This in turn motivates you to engage in activities which will reduce the stress, and/or alter the feelings.

MOOD ALTERATORS
■

If you find yourself taking the same mood alterator three times within a week, ask yourself if you could stop taking it cold turkey. If the answer is "Yes," put yourself to the test and stop taking the alterator for two weeks straight. If after two weeks you want to take it again, go ahead, but keep using the same test on yourself to keep you honest. If the answer is "No," then reach out for some help beyond yourself. Whenever you cannot control when you start, stop, or how much you indulge in an activity, you have become addicted. When you find that you have developed an addiction,

1. Acknowledge it first to yourself
2. Ask yourself what you are willing to do about it

3. Reach out to a friend, a support group, or seek professional help

REFRAMING TO MAKE EVERYTHING RIGHT

One of the ways negaholism displays itself is by focusing on the negative. Recall the story about the glass with a certain amount of water in it. Depending upon how you look at it, it is either half empty or half full.

The art of reframing is an acquired talent. You take the current situation, in which you feel like an innocent victim, and rewrite the incidents so that you appear to be the author of the scenario. You put yourself in the center of the story and make yourself the leading man or woman of the plot. You delete any trace of victim, scapegoat, or martyr from your story. Then you decree that certain incidents happened because you wanted them to happen, almost as if you willed them. Then, finally, you invent reasons which justify your having designed this scene in your movie.

You develop the skill of perceiving situations, events, and circumstances in your life as if they were designed that way. It is as if there were an inherent benefit in every occurrence.

A client named Lisa complained, "I wasted seven years. I moved seven times. I changed jobs seven times. I left a marriage. I couldn't make up my mind. I was shiftless, and unable to make a commitment. I was confused and scattered, and all over the map."

I commented: "How does it make you feel to repeat the past in the tone you conveyed to me?"

She said, "Awful, just awful. I feel like a useless person, and I feel very bad about myself."

I asked her to consider shifting her perspective ever so slightly. She asked for clarification.

I said, "Try this out for size: I was doing exactly what I wanted to be doing every minute of the time. When I had learned the lessons there for me to learn, I moved on to the next learning situation. I experienced an enormous amount, and grew tremendously those seven years. I was experimenting, and experiencing so much of life that I was vital and alive. I never got stuck in any situation; I simply told the truth and moved on. Most of all I was true to myself."

I next asked Lisa if this version was true.

"Yes, but I've never looked at it that way!" she said.

I suggested that she stop finding fault with what she had done in the past and look for the validity in her actions. Then I asked her how she felt after hearing the way I reframed her past history.

"Great! Instead of being the screw-up I became the smart one, the one who made the right decisions."

The argument I hear most frequently about reframing is: "But that's just rationalizing and explaining. What use is that? You're just deceiving yourself. If you really blew it, then learn to live with it. Don't make it into a pious platitude."

My response is simple: Own up to every blunder, mistake, and blooper which you caused or inadvertently made happen; own it, learn the lesson, release it, and move on. In every other case, where you are harping on your "mistakes," reframe and hold the incident as the "right" thing in the overall plan. After all, you're still here, probably no great damage was done, the others survived, and it may have been for the best after all.

A client named Liz lost her father unexpectedly. All the children attended the funeral and afterward learned that their father had written them all out of the will. Liz was devastated. Not only did she have to deal with grief, loss, and sadness, but now confusion, anger, and disillusionment were added to her feelings. For two years she racked her brain trying to figure out why her father had done this, what was he trying to get across? Finally she realized that she was stuck in this incident.

She couldn't move forward in her relationships with men because she simply didn't trust them. She realized that she could either beat herself for something she may have done to alienate her father, or reframe the entire incident and see it as right, appropriate, and just. She worked on this for a long time, and came up with the fact that not having inherited her father's money really empowered her. She didn't have that cushion to depend upon, nor did she rely on anyone else's resources to get her what she wanted in her life. She decided to see the disinheritance as a boon to her self-confidence and her ability to make things happen.

THERE'S GOT TO BE A PONY

■

A story about identical twin boys who were having a birthday exemplifies a point better than anything else I could say. The boys were identical in appearance, but in other ways they were quite different, even opposite. Both boys were very excited and eager to have their presents. Since they were twins, they always received identical gifts. The parents led the first boy blindfolded away from the house and over to his present. The other boy remained back at the house in anticipation. When the first boy got to the present, he looked in front of him and could hardly believe his eyes. He exlaimed, "A barn full of manure! What kind of present is that? Why did you give me that? I deserve better. What an awful present!" And then the first boy hung his head, kicked the dirt, slumped away and sulked off by himself. The parents went back and got the second boy and led him to his present, also blindfolded. When the blindfold was taken off, the second boy jumped for joy, grabbed a shovel and madly started digging. He was excited beyond belief and dug as frantically as you can imagine. The parents asked why he was so excited. He exclaimed, a little out of breath, "There's got to be a pony in here somewhere!"

The moral of the story is that you don't ever have to take anything at face value, things aren't always what they appear, and when life give you manure, instead of seeing it as excrement consider looking at it as fertilizer.

REWRITING
YOUR
CHILDHOOD
■

The next exercise for Lisa was to take every situation in her life where she was dwelling on the negative, half-empty syndrome, and reframe it into being half full. That went for marriages, divorces, disinheritances, embezzlement, terminated relationships, and so on.

Lisa asked if she weren't merely justifying her past actions, and ultimately creating a sugar-coating around the reality of the past.

I responded by asking her if the second twin's reaction was any less valid than that of the first.

When she said no, it wasn't, I posited that every situation has two sides to it, and one can choose either perspective. It really doesn't matter which perspective you choose, because both are true. What matters is how you view yourself.

Lisa argued that this was what criminals did after they had committed crimes, justifying in their minds what they had done.

Admitting to the possibility, I went on to explain to her that I was not advocating she do this exercise with reference to anything which was illegal, immoral, unethical, or against the golden rule. There are certain actions for which we should feel guilt and shame, primarily acts that hurt others or society. I am not suggesting that this guilt or shame should be permanent, or that forgiveness and absolution for wrongdoings is not highly desirable if you are to live a healthy life. Unlike Hester Prynne in *The Scarlet Letter*, you do not have to wear a red A on your chest for the rest of your days.

The exercise of reframing is useful for those choices and decisions in your life which you have judged as "bad" or "wrong," held against yourself, and used as evidence to build a case indicting yourself as unable, unworthy, undesirable, or unlovable. As a psychologist and dear friend of mine, Jamie Weinstein, puts it, "It's never too late to have a happy childhood!"

The real value of the reframing exercise is that it shifts your perspective from half empty to half full. You can then release yourself from the guilt, remorse, and punishment of having made the wrong choice or having done "it" wrong, and affirm yourself for being the star that you already are. This concept was so difficult for Lisa to grasp that she contested even more loudly, claiming that this went against everything she had been taught about management. She said if she didn't take herself in hand when she did something "wrong" and address it properly so that she learned from her mistakes, she would probably do it again. It became apparent to me that we really needed to get to the bottom of this issue or she would never accept this concept. I started to give her a minicourse in motivation. There are many ways to motivate youself and others. I am going to explain two different approaches.

MANAGEMENT
BY
FEAR
■

The first way is to motivate using the "stick" method. In this approach, you try to get yourself or others to produce the result you want by using coercion, threats, and fear of the consequences.

In this form of management there is usually an inherent power struggle which results in forced compliance. The target complies with the wishes of the "manager" because of fear of the consequences, which is usually associated with punish-

ment. This is called deprivation motivation, management by
fear or consequence management.

Phrases associated with this approach are, "If you don't,
I'll . . . ," "You'd better do it, or else . . . ," and "If you want to
go to the party, then you'd better . . ." The results from this
approach are usually effective for the short term. You get the
person to comply with your wishes, but they are going along
with your demands to avoid unpleasant consequences, not because they want to.

MANAGEMENT
BY
PARTICIPATION
■

In this approach, one employs "reinforcement theory." You first
find out what people want: their preferences. Then you enable
them to pursue their wants in an environment which provides
them with timely, relevant, and meaningful feedback. Every
time people perform the behavior that you desire, you reinforce
them in some positive and tangible way so that the behavior
is repeated. Positive reinforcement is saying to yourself or another, "Good girl, do this again. This is desirable behavior. We
want more of this!"

SELF-MANAGEMENT
■

Now let's get specific, focusing on your relationship with yourself. You can "manage" yourself with threats and cruelty
(which is probably familiar to you). In that case, you probably
have some underlying assumptions about yourself: You're lazy,
and/or don't want to work and need to be cajoled, coerced, or
forced into getting the job done. This perspective will make

you act like a critical parent who is continually having to discipline a naughty child, one who keeps trying to get out of her chores and/or act out. This is a full-time job.

Motivating, disciplining, complaining about, being mean to, prophesying about, and ultimately being right about this pain in the neck takes up a lot of time and energy. In effect, you are practicing reinforcement theory, but in reverse. You are reinforcing your own negative behavior. You are shining the spotlight on the negative aspects and you are eliciting more of the same behavior. It is as if you have your own set of grow lights and whatever you focus on becomes bigger than life.

MOTIVATION
THROUGH
CHOICE
■

There is a totally different approach to inner-directed motivation. The new approach is motivation through choice. Using this approach to manage yourself requires close attention. It means putting the vision of what you want to have in your life in front of yourself. You manage yourself through reinforcement of the positive, not avoidance of the negative. The approach is gentle, caring, and nurturing. You are kind and encouraging with your every move. You interact with yourself in such a positive way that you want to be close to you because it feels so good.

1. Examine your feelings, sorting out the myriad of different ones you have within.
2. Determine what you really want. Not so much your ego, your appetites, or your internal voices, but rather your essential self.
3. Allow yourself to become inspired about your secret wishes, hopes, and dreams.
4. Hold all these aspirations within the realm of possi-

bility, believing that you can truly have what you
want.

5. Reinforce yourself constantly and consistently with acknowledgments, pats on the cheek, etc.

6. Validate every step forward in the direction you desire.

7. Keep the inspiration alive and close to your heart.

8. Stick with it, believing in yourself and in the dream,
no matter what.

9. Build a support team of personal cheerleaders, to build
you up when you get discouraged.

10. Celebrate when you achieve the desired end result.

THE BEATER-METER

■

To show you how this phenomenon works, I will ask you to
either recall (if you are old enough) or imagine (if you are not),
a TV program entitled *Queen for a Day*. This was aired back
in the fifties and hosted by a man named Jack Bailey. The show
presented three women who each had a sob story, each one
being more desperate and heartrending than the next. After
hearing all the stories, the audience would determine who
would be "Queen for a Day." The studio audience voted on the
women's stories by applauding loudest and longest for the one
who seemed the most in need. The applause was recorded on
an applause meter that filled the entire screen.

This is relevant because you have your own personal applause meter inside your head. This is both good news and bad
news. The good news is that you have a automatic internal
gauge: Hooray! The bad news is that the gauge cannot distinguish between positive and negative attention. It is a faulty
gauge. It cannot discriminate between applause and boos, bra-
vos and flying tomatoes. It just hears noise. The louder the
better. The applause meter can turn into a beater-meter. Now
let's look at specific examples in your life.

* * *

EXAMPLE #1 You made your bed. What does the applause/ beater-meter say: zero. The voice commentary says, "Big deal. You are *always* supposed to make your bed. No points!"

EXAMPLE #2 You completed a project of mailing out twenty-five letters to constituents. Applause/beater-meter registers: zero. The voice commentary says: "It's about time! You were supposed to get that project done two weeks ago. Finally it's complete."

EXAMPLE #3 You completed a piece of research that has been hanging over your head. Applause/beater-meter registers: zero. The voice commentary says, "Now you can write the paper you have been procrastinating on for so long, and just think of the ten other projects that are waiting when you finish that one!"

Now maybe zero is underestimating you, and you are more positive than you seem. Perhaps you would have given yourself 10, maybe 25, or even 37 for anyone of these. If you gave yourself over 50 on any one of them, you are in pretty good shape. Now let's change the stimuli ever so slightly.

EXAMPLE #1 You left your bedroom a mess, the bed is unmade, the clothes are all over the room, papers and magazines scattered on the dresser. The applause/beater-meter registers: 25. The voice commentary says, "Look at this mess! You are such a slob! You can't find a thing, just look at this pigsty!"

EXAMPLE #2 You have succeeded in getting 2 out of the 25 letters out for the mailing and a month has elapsed. Applause/beater-meter registers: 45. The voice commentary says, "I can't believe that you can't get 25 measly letters in the mail. It's not that big a deal! Why are you making it into a major project. This is ridiculous! You are simply hopeless!"

EXAMPLE #3 You are three months behind in the research project that you need to do, with no end in sight. The deadline has come and gone, and each day your boss asks you about the project. You feel anxious, guilty, fearful, worried, and panicky about ever getting the project accomplished. Furthermore there is no action plan to ensure completion. The applause/beater-meter registers: 75. The voice commentary says, "You never should have agreed to do this research. You know that you hate research. You knew going in that you would never do it. Why did you agree to a project that you would never do? How stupid! You will agree to anything that you are asked to do, just to be nice and have everybody like you. Now you're trapped, and there is no way out. Everyone is going to know that you don't know what you are doing. You are going to look like an idiot. Everyone is going to hate you because you are letting them down. YOU are the weak link in the machine. How embarrassing! Will you ever learn? God, you are so dumb!"

Let's throw in one more for good luck.

EXAMPLE #4 Let's just say that you left your keys locked in the car. Applause/beater-meter: 100. Voice commentary, "YOU MORON! I HAVE NEVER SEEN SUCH AN IMBECILE IN ALL MY LIFE! WHAT WERE YOU THINKING OF? AND WITH THE CAR RUNNING, NO LESS?"

Do you hear how you are managing yourself? When you exhibit behaviors that are desirable, you respond in an off-handed, casual manner, assuming that you are expected to behave this way. If a behavior is expected, you act as if it need not be recognized or reinforced.

When you exhibit behaviors that are undesirable, you become a taskmaster, criticizing, judging, faultfinding, and belittling yourself. Your applause/beater-meter is sending a signal to your brain which says, "Do more of this behavior, because the response is registering high." Remember, it doesn't know the difference between positive and negative applause/beating (attention). All it registers is noise. It registers whatever volume it hears as recognition. Each time this happens, a mental note is made which says, "This is a good one, do more of this."

You have successfully placed yourself between a rock and a hard place. You can't win for losing. When do you ever really get positive recognition? Rarely, if ever; or never. The assumption is: Keep pushing and driving, don't give her any pats on the back or she'll get cocky and fall down on the job. Give 'em an inch and they'll take a mile.

In order to reverse this process you need to behave in a very unfamiliar manner. You need to make a big deal out of the things that you have accomplished, no matter how insignificant they may be. At the same time you need to minimize the recognition of behaviors which are undesirable. In other words, you don't give your screwups a lot of attention. You notice them, but you do not shine the spotlight on them or put them on the P.A. system. Notice means observe, and simply that.

"HMMMMMMMMMMMMMMMM"

It sounds like, "Hmmmmmm, isn't it interesting that I am resisting handling my correspondence? I wonder why I am doing that. What can I learn about myself from this behavior? What can I do to remedy the situation? What do I need in order to get this task accomplished? Is there anything I need in the long term/big picture which will alleviate this situation in the future?" or "Hmmmmmm, I notice that I am not getting my project written, and it's now past due. There must be something going on here that I can learn from. Instead of getting upset at either the situation or myself, I think I'd rather learn something which would benefit me in future situations like this. Now, let's examine this one thoroughly. Initially I wanted to do the project. Time has passed and it has become prioritized several times because of other more pressing matters. I think I need to book time slots into my calendar in order to get it done. Secondly, I am overwhelmed with the amount of data which I need to read and absorb in order to complete this project. I think I need to break it down into bite-size pieces, and incorporate the pieces into the already-booked time in the calendar. I will execute these two steps now."

The difference between using the applause/beater-meter to your advantage and having it go haywire has to do with managing your resources and having them work for you. Learning from your behavior is very different from slamming yourself for not doing what you said you would do. You need to get your strokes from behaviors which move you in the direction that you want to be going, and simply notice, strategize, and learn from those behaviors which are off track.

SELF-TRUST
■

The question is: How do you feel about yourself? Probably not like the superstar that you are. You may feel guilty, sad, remorseful, like a failure, and even a little hopeless. The end result is that when you treat yourself like this, you drive a wedge between you and your essential self, you become "at two" instead of "at one." You can tell if you are "at two" if there is a running dialogue in your head. If you are "at one," it is quiet inside.

Each time you do this, you erode the trust that you feel for yourself. Your essential self starts to resemble a battered child, afraid to make a decision because he is going to get clobbered for whatever you choose. In order to foster self-trust, you need to stop beating yourself up. Period.

You cannot beat yourself and trust yourself simultaneously. It is simply not possible for these two antithetical realities to coexist.

Self-trust is the core of self-confidence and decision making. If you do not trust yourself, then you cannot be expected to feel confident in what you think, what you feel, or what you want. Therefore, you spend most of your life in indecision, looking to others for their input, advice, and feedback regardless of whether you ultimately use it or not.

After they give you their advice, you are never sure whether you should follow it or not, since you cannot determine whether they are right or wrong. After much consternation—sometimes weeks, months, or even years—you make up your mind what to do, but you are never really sure if you made the right decision. After the decision is made, you hedge your bet, and wait to see how it turns out. Sure enough, you made the wrong decision again! "How could you!" And so it goes.

The process of self-validation is a way of affirming the positive side of yourself. Instead of taking things for granted and acting bored and blasé, you celebrate the little wins of life and make a big deal out of them. The reason that you act in this silly, almost contrived way is to:

- reinforce that you can be trusted
- back the previous choices that you have made
- give you confidence to make the next decision
- build and reinforce your essential self's inner sense of right and wrong

WHAT TO DO WHEN THE TRUST IS GONE

■

Trust is fragile. It can be developed or eroded. Trust is believing that something is true, or believing in someone's word. When you tell yourself that you're going to do something and you don't keep your word, you have just diminished your trust level with yourself. Each time you break your promise to yourself, you chip away at the supply of trust. For instance, suppose you say, with the best of intentions, that you are going to get up every morning and work out at the gym, and then the first morning you wake up and feel tired and say, "I'm too tired. I'll work out later." When "later" comes, you still don't go to the gym, but this time you say, "I'll go tomorrow morning." When tomorrow morning comes you think, "I have too much to do. I'll go this weekend." And so on. The fourth time you say you will go to the gym, what is your response? You may start hearing, "Sure you will, just like the last time. You're not going to go to the gym. You'll end up sleeping in like you usually do. Who do you think you're kidding?" When you say you'll do something and you don't do it, you erode your self-trust. You put one more notch in the holster which says your word doesn't count for much. The next time you promise yourself that you will go to the gym, since you haven't built a track record of times when you *have* gone, you have no defense against this barrage. After all, it's true. What can you say?

There is, however, a way out of this negative-trust corkscrew. The resolution doesn't happen overnight; after all, the erosion didn't happen overnight, either. It is a process that takes time. The process of rebuilding trust is similar to eroding trust, one step at a time. Each time you have a choice to make a commitment to yourself, look very carefully and see if you can keep your promise. Start with little promises, ones you know you can keep. Commit to brushing your teeth, and then do it. Commit to calling a specific person, and then do it. Start with baby steps, and build one block at a time. Focus on the process of rebuilding your self-trust rather than accomplishing the result.

Mary constantly broke promises to herself. She would commit to never eat sugar again. Sure enough, the next time she went out to dinner and the waiter brought over the dessert tray, she would give in. The beat-ups were brutal. I pointed out that she was setting herself up for a losing game. Every time she wanted to change a behavior, she might want to commit to mini-units of time rather than forever. For instance, perhaps she could commit to not having sugar tonight, and then tomorrow have a chance to examine whether she wants to renew the commitment. "Forever" seemed an incomprensible time to Mary, so she would think, "Oh, one little dessert won't hurt. If I'm making this commitment for the rest of my life, then just tonight doesn't matter." She would sabotage herself with her own logic.

Don't make agreements that you can't keep. If you can absolutely keep your promise, then make the commitment. After you have kept your promise, validate yourself for reinstating a portion of your self-trust, for doing what you said. If you feel that you cannot keep the commitment, then don't make it. It is better to make fewer commitments and keep the ones that you make than make too many and break them. Remember, your self-trust is at stake. It is easily broken and hard to repair.

BUILDING
A
CASE LIST
■

An exercise that you can do to reinforce self-trust is the following: On paper, perhaps in your journal, make a *Building a Case List*. This list is to be referred to whenever self-doubt or fear threaten to take over. It is comprised of times when you did what you said you would do, times when you won, times when you were a hero, or a star, or any time when you lived up to the expectations that you set for yourself. Trust comes out of having the confidence or belief that you or others will do what you say. To build self-trust, you need to believe your own words, to feel that your words are gold. You need to know that you can count on you. You need to feel in your heart that you won't let you down.

MOTIVATION
BY ASPIRING
TO BE
YOUR BEST SELF
■

The choice of how to manage yourself is yours. You can revert to your old behavior and be cruel, managing yourself with threats, coercion, and fear, or you can choose a new way of operating. You can motivate yourself by aspiring to be your best self. This is not coming from fear of the consequences, slave driving, or the need for disciplining. The new management style presupposes that you are a worthwhile person who is capable, willing, and eager to contribute once the right motivator is found.

- Choose the behaviors that you want to reinforce; being neat, accomplishing tasks, doing what you say you will do, being on time, exercising, eating foods that are desirable for you to have in order to get the body that you want, getting your paperwork done in time, getting your bills paid on time, getting your projects done ahead of schedule. Whatever they are.
- Write them all down on a piece of paper, and determine an appropriate positive response/applause for the behavior when you have demonstrated it.
- Make a pact with yourself that when you don't live up to the behavior expectation you have set for yourself, you will respond with, "Hmmmmmmm, isn't that interesting that I didn't———." This is merely an observation of fact, and not an indictment. There needn't be any judgment attached to the comment.
- "Hmmmmmm" is a tone, not a thought. The tone will stimulate the right side of the brain and not the left side, which is analytical. The point is to notice the behavior so that you can change it, not to make a big deal out of it so that you reinforce it.

THE
FORGIVENESS
LETTER
■

This exercise works for people who are ready to heal the past. It is not for those with deep-seated resentments, wounds, and hurts, which need more in-depth processing. This exercise is mainly for you to use with yourself, but you can also use it in relationship to other people in your life.

Forgiveness is a very powerful tool. When you are engaged in an inner struggle and you feel distance between you and yourself, it is time to make amends. You have the power and the ability to absolve yourself from the wrong that's been done. By writing yourself an official document which releases you from the guilt which you would inflict upon yourself, you can repair the damage.

For those situations in your life that require forgiveness, use this exercise.

Find a quiet place and some time to yourself when you won't be interrupted. Bring with you a tablet and a pen. Write yourself a letter that starts like this:

Dear ———,
On this ——— day, of ——— (month) in ——— (year), I am officially extending to you absolution and forgiveness for these offenses [here list every thought, action, and deed which you have been harboring against yourself].

At the end of the letter write the following:

I have the authority to extend to you amnesty and forgiveness for all of the above. From this day forward these issues shall be wiped from your record, and will nevermore be used against you. You start this day with a clean slate, with no transgressions against you. You are a free person, free from guilt, and self-recrimination. Go, and live your life a free person, who will treat yourself and others with respect, dignity, and positive regard. Congratulations!

Then sign the letter.

Read this letter aloud to yourself in a clear and robust voice. You can then either burn it or frame it and put it on the wall.

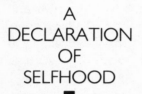

A DECLARATION OF SELFHOOD

Virginia Satir was one of the great family therapists of our time; I had the privilege of knowing her and her work personally. One of her tools was a personal "Bill of Rights," which is a claiming of your birthright. You can photocopy this list and put it on your mirror in the bathroom and read it to yourself every day while you are brushing your hair. Say it out loud to yourself. Listen to your voice grow in strength and volume so that you really start to feel it inside. In the beginning, you may feel silly or embarrassed. You may hear the inner voice say, "That's not the truth." Just hang in there and keep doing it; you'll notice changes within six weeks, if you do it religiously. Here is the list. Try it out, you'll like it, give it a chance.

BILL OF RIGHTS, BY VIRGINIA SATIR

■

1. I do not have to feel guilty just because someone else does not like what I do, say, think, or feel.
2. It is O.K. for me to feel angry and to express it in responsible ways.
3. I do not have to assume full responsibility for making decisions, particularly where others share responsibility for making the decisions.
4. I have the right to say "I don't understand" without feeling stupid or guilty.
5. I have the right to say "I don't know."
6. I have the right to say NO without feeling guilty.
7. I do not have to apologize or give reasons when I say NO.
8. I have the right to ask others to do things for me.
9. I have the right to refuse requests which others make of me.
10. I have the right to tell others when I think they are manipulating, conning, or treating me unfairly.
11. I have the right to refuse additional responsibilities without feeling guilty.
12. I have the right to tell others when their behavior annoys me.
13. I do not have to compromise my personal integrity.
14. I have the right to make mistakes and to be responsible for them. I have the right to be wrong.
15. I do not have to be liked, admired, or respected by everyone for everything I do.

RITUALIZING
EVENTS
■

Burning, framing, exhibiting, and celebrating, are various forms of ritualization. These forms of ritualizing will imprint the experience on your brain so that you will "experience" the event. Conceptualizing information is not the same as experiencing it. Very often you need to dramatize and/or ritualize events to intensify their impact.

The reason we have rites of passage is to ritualize important events, so that we realize that something significant has transpired. This affects our internal perception of reality. Rituals around birth, entering a religious denomination, entering puberty, marriage, anniversaries, celebrating successes, the passage of one year to another, death, and so on permit us to record in our central nervous system that there has been a major change. If you didn't ritualize, you would know intellectually that something was different, but it wouldn't be "real" to you. Think of rituals which you have missed (i.e., the funeral of a dear friend), and notice how many times you acted as if that person were still alive, as if you hadn't internalized it. The purpose of ritualizing is to bring the reality of the event home to you so it is real.

MIND
DIALOGUING
TO GET
OFF THE FENCE
■

Have you ever noticed those times when you can't make up your mind? Should I stay in bed, or go jogging? Should I go out with George or with David? Should I go with the new job offer or stay where I am? Should I keep my old car or should I buy a new one? Does this sound familiar?

Indecision is an indication of some subtle form of mental cruelty accompanied by never-ending ongoing dialogue between you and yourself. Let's take as an example the decision to buy a new car or keep the old one. A client named Mary actually went through this dialogue right in my office.

> "I can't make up my mind. Should I sell my car, and buy or lease a new one, or should I just keep the old one?"

I asked her to tell me her reasons: pro and con.

She said, "I think I should get a new car because I have had my car four years, and I would get the best resale value at this time; but on the other hand, a new car is really expensive. If I sold my car, I would avoid repair problems that occur with cars as they get older, but on the other hand my car has only 43,000 miles on it, which is great for a car four years old. I think it would be fun to have a new car, but I don't really need one. I have just recently had a new clutch put in and I had mechanical difficulties with the convertible top, but on the other hand these are small problems and I really haven't had much trouble with the car in the past. A new car would eliminate all concerns about maintenance and repairs, but what if I got a lemon, that would be awful!"

She went on and on, until I said, "What do you want to do?"

"I don't know!," Mary replied.

I said to her, "It sounds like whatever you choose will probably be the wrong choice. The great guillotine in the sky is waiting to cut off your head if you make the wrong choice."

"That's exactly right, so for weeks I have been stuck not being able to make up my mind."

I told her that I wanted to teach her a technique called mind dialoguing.

Mind dialoguing is a process whereby you have a conversation with your mind for the purpose of quieting the voices, attaining some quiet in your mind, and then allowing yourself to embark upon the adventure of choosing. Mind dialoguing goes like this: When you hear the familiar refrain in your mind, you simply choose one side, it doesn't matter which one, and agree with it. After you do this several times, the voices cease, and then you can ask yourself, "What do I want?"

The purpose of the exercise is to quiet the voices of the mind so that you can have silence in which to ask the important question. When you have silence, you can invoke the intuitive part of yourself in order to get a sense about what to do. Given the previous examples, take the part that says: I want to get a new car. Take this side only, and forget about all the "on the other hands."

TO
PLAY
THIS OUT
■

You say, "I think I should get a new car, because I have had my car four years, and I would get the best resale value at this time."

I then say, "Yeah, you probably should."

You say, "If I sold my car, I would avoid repair problems that occur with cars as they get older."

I say, "That's true."

You say, "I think it would be fun to have a new car."

I say, "It would."

You say, "A new car would eliminate all concerns about maintenance and repairs."

I say, "Uh huh, sure enough" and so on.

"So what has happened to you?" I asked Mary, after we'd gone through this.

Mary said, "Everything got quiet inside. But is that my choice?"

"No," I responded. "You have merely taken step one, which

is quieting the voices. This is not the end result, which is making a choice which feels good to you inside."

"What if we reversed our roles and I took the other side: to keep my old car, then what?" asked Mary.

I said, "Let's do it and see what happens. You go first."

> Mary said, "My car has only 43,000 miles on it, which is great for a car four years old."
>
> I said, "That's true."
>
> She said, "I don't really need a new car."
>
> "No, you don't," I said.
>
> "What if I got a lemon!" she exclaimed.
>
> "That could happen, you know," I said.
>
> "I have really had no problems with the car in the past," Mary said.
>
> "You haven't," I commented.
>
> And so on . . .

"What did you notice, Mary?" I inquired.

"The voices stopped, just like the previous time."

"Now, listen very carefully when I ask this question: Do you want to keep your present car or buy a new one?"

Immediately she responded, "Buy a new one, that's all there is to it. It is clear. I want a new car!" She was delighted to have resolved the issue and be able to move on to something else.

In order to resolve mental gymnastics which go nowhere except along the same treadmill, follow these simple steps:

1. Identify the two opposing issues
2. Write or talk it out into a tape recorder
3. Choose one side, either one
4. Run the dialogue either in writing or orally, but only do one side of the mind
5. Agree with everything that you say
6. When the voices stop, ask yourself, "What do I want?"
7. Listen to the answer and write it down

8. If you don't believe it, do it with the other side of your mind
9. If you don't get an answer, do it again until you do
10. When you get your answer, celebrate and acknowledge yourself

JOURNAL KEEPING

■

Another technique which works really well, especially when you are alone, is journal keeping. This technique works when you have an altercation with a loved one and there is no one else to talk to, or when you are traveling and you are alone with your thoughts, or simply any time when you want to check inside and take your mental-health pulse. It is a way in which to tune in to yourself, get into communication and sort out what is going on inside. Eric was a prime example for whom journal keeping worked beautifully.

A concerned Eric sat in the armchair in my office. He was recounting the latest developments in his relationship with Sandy. He said, "Everything seems to be working between us."

Eric originally came to see me because of a business-related issue. Shortly after we clarified his objectives for the consulting work, he discovered that he had similar problems in both his business and his personal relationships. He said, "I am not certain what to do about it, but I seem to be totally out of touch with my feelings. Every time Sandy asks me how and/ or what I am feeling I automatically respond with what I am thinking, without knowing it. She has pointed it out to me, and she's right. What can I do to start to find, feel, notice my feelings? Can you help me with this kind of an issue?"

I suggested to Eric that he begin to keep a journal. He asked how that would help. I told him it was a way to record internal thoughts and begin to probe below the surface and start searching for feelings.

"You can use the journal as a sort of divining rod rooting around in search of your true feelings." I then began to give him some of the primary reasons for the journal-keeping process:

- to get to know your mind and how it works
- to begin to uncover your feelings and sort them out
- to view your internal process from an objective perspective

When you see your innermost thoughts and feelings on paper before your eyes, it can alter your perception of reality. In other words, you can begin to separate yourself from your thoughts, feelings, ideas, and condition. The journal is not like the diary you may have used in childhood. That treasured book was a tool in which you would record facts, events, and conversations. This journal is primarily a tool for self-discovery. It can be used as a receptacle for mind chatter. It can be used as a tool to listen to yourself. It can also be a valuable mirror in which to see yourself in a new light or from a different angle. Very often you are unaware of the underlying beliefs or decisions which govern your attitudes and behavior. Listening through the written words can enable you to unlock patterns which you might otherwise obscure from yourself. You can also use the journal as a validation tool. You can record your "pats on the back" in your journal to highlight accomplishments and achievements.

There is no right way to keep your journal. I can offer some advice to help you get the most out of the journalizing experience:

Record your *feelings*, reactions, and thoughts. Focus on your internal experience.

Tell your truth to the best of your ability. Then dig deeper and see if there is some even deeper truth. Ask yourself questions like:

- "What is the truth about that?"
- "Is there something even deeper?"
- "What is the truth about that?"

Listen and write down whatever answers you receive. Use the journal to get to the bottom of issues which surface. In doing this, you will create conditions for a catharsis which will release the emotion on an issue or an incident.

Whenever possible, use your journal in the midst of conflict—when you are having a quarrel with a loved one and you are at your wit's end, for instance. Both of you think that you are right and you are at an impasse. Take your journal and write down all the feelings you can get in touch with, and keep digging deeper to see what is really underneath it all. When your emotions are the closest to the surface, you can use your journal as a tool to peel back the layers of thoughts and surface feelings to see what is *really* going on. Anger often masks the more vulnerable feelings which lurk in the shadows of our emotional fabric. On the surface you are obviously angry. When you dig down, you may discover hurt, sadness, and even some other tender feelings. This is a very effective way to use the journal.

When you feel out of sorts and don't know why, use the journal to externalize whatever is there. Don't worry about it making sense or being responsible; write whatever you observe, think, feel, sense, or judge.

Forget about punctuation, grammar, syntax, and spelling. No one is going to read your journal but you, so tell it like it is. Make sure that it is legible so that you can read it later, but don't edit, rehearse, censor, or withhold.

Have your journal be a safe place for you. You can tell it all your most hidden expectations, fears, wishes, hopes, and dreams. You are the only one who will ever know. You can expand upon your fantasies, fears, frolics, or fun. You can tell your visions, plans, hurts, and joys.

Use your journal daily. Set aside a special time every day to write in it, or carry it around with you and use it on and off throughout the day. Even if you have nothing to say, write down that you have nothing to say, but don't go a day without writing. Make this commitment to yourself, and follow it through.

NURTURES

■

A very bright and loving publishing executive was caught in a dilemma.

Jimmy said to me one sunny morning. "I love my work; I love my wife; I love my kids, but I don't really know if I even like myself."

I asked him what gave him this suspicion.

"I would do anything for them," he said.

I asked him to be specific.

He said, "I call my wife once, sometimes twice a day, sometimes just to say I love her. I buy her flowers, usually once a week. I leave her notes around the house, in the refrigerator, or on her car seat that say I am thinking of her. I make sure that we have at least one evening each week that is special; a night when we get dressed up for each other, go out to dinner, maybe even dancing. We leave the kids at home and we embark on a romantic evening of courting and flirting with each other."

I said, "I'm almost jealous; she's a very fortunate woman. But what about the kids?"

"Oh it's the same story, I take them to ball games, the movies, help them with their homework. Hell, I even took them river rafting this summer. They know I love them, and, in fact, I do."

I asked him what behavior or actions conveyed the message.

"I care, I make them a priority," he said. "I spend time with them. I am there to hear their problems. I am genuinely interested. And last but not least, I spend money on them."

"Really," I said. "Through the allocation of time, energy, and money you demonstrate to your wife and children that they are important to you?"

"That's right!" he said.

"Now," I said, "let's turn to your relationship with yourself. What do you do to demonstrate to yourself that you care about you?" He thought for several minutes.

"Nothing, absolutely nothing!"

"I said, "There must be something you do. Think about it. Exercise, maybe?"

He replied, "Oh sure, I exercise, but that's to keep in shape; I do that for my health."

I said, "You're always well groomed, what about the personal care you take with your appearance?"

He retorted, "I do that because it's part of my professional image. I need to do that for my job."

I began to explain to Jimmy that many of his actions, if framed differently, could be construed as caring gestures rather than merely functional ones. "I want you to use your relationship with your wife as a model of how you want to relate to yourself. Just like sending her flowers, leaving her notes, or planning an evening out, you know exactly what to do to make her feel special. You also know what to do to have your kids feel cared about."

What do you like to do? What makes you feel cared about? What makes you feel worthwhile? What could someone do to have you feel special? This list is very important in helping to build the relationship that you say you want with yourself. You need to have the care and concern demonstrated in actions so that you *feel* them. The first step is to make a nurturing list of special things you could do for yourself.

Nurtures are a specific way to counterbalance all the times you take yourself for granted. A nurture is a tangible way to communicate and to demonstrate to yourself from yourself that you care about yourself. It is a demonstration to show that you are willing to take the time, to spend the money, to allocate the energy to let you know that you matter, that you are worth it. Use your five senses to feed your soul. There are certain textures, colors, fragrances, sounds, and tastes which touch a cord deep inside and make you feel special. They are unique to you, and if you search, you will, with very little effort, become aware of what they are. If you make a list, it will always be available for those moments when you cannot think of what to do to care for yourself.

Some nurtures might be:

- lying in the sun
- watching the sunset
- sleeping in
- having breakfast in bed
- writing in your journal
- jogging
- taking a bubble bath
- getting a massage
- playing with your children
- horseback riding
- going out to eat
- going to the movies
- doing a favorite sport
- going dancing

You put together your own list of nurtures, activities that resonate to you, that say to you: "you're special," "I like you," "you are important to me," "you are worth it." Nurtures are a way to transcend words and demonstrate what you want to communicate to yourself. You will be pleasantly surprised when you actively treat yourself to a nurture and see how you feel. It is similar to having a lover who is doting on you and saying in various ways: "I love you!" As special as nurtures are, there are two pitfalls to be avoided:

- The first is to go through the motions of nurturing yourself automatically, without ritualizing it. For example you say to yourself in a blasé, offhand manner, "I guess I'll get a massage." You make a joyful experience into a mundane, routine task. Rather than experiencing the physical pleasure and joy of receiving a gift, you go through the motions because you know you should nurture yourself. You forget to let in the experience of receiving, of being cared for and about. A nurture is meant to be nourishing.
- Cheap thrills, mentioned in Chapter Three, occur when your mind is being deceptive and tells you that you *de-*

serve a nurture. You then select something which has the appearance of a nurture but which is really a beat-up in disguise. An example of a cheap thrill is eating a hot fudge sundae when you are on a diet, or spending the rent money on a new pair of boots, then not having the money when the rent is due. At the time, they feel like nurtures, but lurking in the background is a way to "get" yourself.

THE STANDARD/ REALITY GAP

■

After I'd discussed all this with Jimmy, he exclaimed, "I don't think I am ever going to stop beating myself up! Maybe, Chérie, I'll be your first failure. After all, this stuff is not foolproof. There has to be one fluke in the bunch, and I guess I'm it!"

"Not so fast, Jimmy," I answered, "If you have resigned yourself to being the exception, there is nothing I can do but let you be just that. However, if you are willing to give it another go, we can try a different tack. What do you say?"

"I'm skeptical," he said, "but willing, so let's get to it."

"Some people are really hard on themselves," I said. "The way they are cruel to themselves is by setting unattainable goals and then saying, 'I told you so!' when they don't achieve the goal. It gets even more insidious than that. The goal becomes tangled and confused into an all-pervasive standard, which is perceived as 'the way I am supposed to be,' and which is vastly different from the way they are. I happen to think, Jimmy, that you suffer from this version of self-flagellation."

Continually comparing the reality of their situation to the unreal standard (the way they are supposed to be), self-flagellators use the discrepancy between the two as ammunition for beat-up. See the chart on page 177.

STANDARD/REALITY MODEL

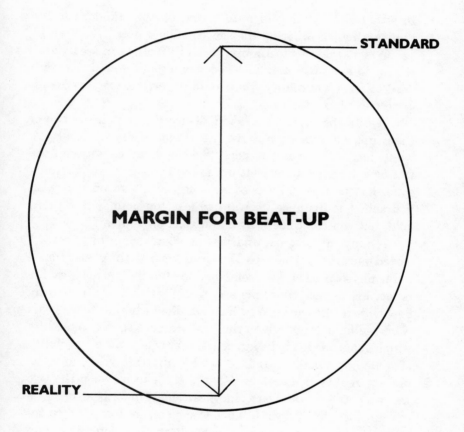

STANDARD

MARGIN FOR BEAT-UP

REALITY

There are two ways to eliminate this ammunition or source of beat-up:

- You can either move the reality to meet the standard or,
- You can move the standard to meet the reality.

In either case, your goal is to match up the standard to the reality, thus eliminating the source of beat-up.

When I told this to Jimmy, he said, "Well, I can see moving reality to meet the standard, because if you lowered the standard to meet the reality, you would never challenge yourself, or strive for excellence."

"Quite the contrary," I said. "Once you match the two of them up, you can then move the standard to any level you want, just as long as you don't use the distance between the two as your margin for beat-up. It can be used as your stretch zone, but it musn't be used as ammunition to open fire on yourself. For instance, to want to lose ten pounds is a great goal, but you can't use it as a bludgeon on yourself."

Jimmy understood, and we set about examining his assorted margins for beat-ups. He wrote down all the goals related to his physical body, his profession, his family, his hobbies, his home, his leisure time, his secret aspirations, and generally how he is in the world. We then examined whether these goals were realistic or not, given the time frames. Then I asked him which goals needed to be altered so that there was a possibility of matching up the standard set by him (his goal), and the present reality. I mentioned that if the gap between the two was wide, there would be a significant margin for beat-up. This margin for beat-up would be seized upon by his mind to invalidate his progress and even his best intentions. Our aim was to set up a winnable game which would eliminate any margin for self-torment.

Remember Sam, the minister's son? This is how the standard/reality model relates to him. The *standard* which had been set by Sam's family was to be the minister's son. Sam was supposed to deny all worldy pleasures, practice self-denial and self-sacrifice. The *reality* of the situation was that Sam wanted everything hedonistic and material that he could get his hands on. The discrepancy between the standard and the reality was his margin for self-torment. Since he couldn't live up to the standard which had been set for him by his parents, and he felt it wasn't O.K. to want what he wanted, he could *never* have what he wanted. In order for the cruelty, or the negaholism, to go away, he would have to bring the standard and the reality into alignment.

Either he would have to live his life according to the standard set and move the reality to the standard, or he would have to claim his right to want and have what he wanted without guilt. He would then move the standard to become the reality. As it was, he was trapped in never being able to be O.K., never measuring up or fulfilling either his parents' desires or his own. Caught between the two, his only recourse was to

- find a mood alterator to escape the reality
- be cruel to himself in the margin for self-torment indefinitely

Negaholism is being trapped in the margin for beat-up zone, being told over and over again that you can't be, do, or have what you want. There are some specific and consistent similarities which underlie all addictive behavior.

THE PUNCHING-BAG RELATIONSHIP
■

One of the ways that addictions manifest themselves is in the area of relationships. It is always nice to have a friend, a companion, a special person to spend time with. Too often what seems to happen is that we use that special person as one of those inflatable clowns with sand in the base. We punch at the clown and it bounces back, so we punch harder. The game gets to be "punch the clown." We may find ourselves in relationships which seem like "punching the clown." The relationship is a beat-up, but we can't get out of it.

THE
HALL OF
MIRRORS
IN RELATIONSHIPS
■

As long as you have not accepted your own individuality, uniqueness, strengths, and weaknesses, it will be difficult if not impossible to accept those differences in another person. The other person reflects back, magnified and in Technicolor, those parts of you which you have not accepted. They don't need to be identical. It works like this: If you can't stand the fact that he is watching TV, then maybe you never give yourself permission for leisure time. The fact that he is lying around unproductive while you are driven to stay busy drives you crazy. Every time something about the other person gets under your skin, you can probably discover something valuable about your relationship with yourself.

As they look in the hall of mirrors, each person is faced with two possible options:

- judge and criticize the other person for his shortcomings or
- come to terms with the feelings of inadequacy, loneliness, fear of abandonment, and fear of entrapment which keep you estranged.

LET THINGS
AND PEOPLE BE
WHO AND
WHAT THEY ARE
■

Have you ever heard yourself saying, "Oh, I wish he were taller," or "If only he were more affectionate," or "I wish she weren't so moody," or "If only she understood my pressures and how hard it is for me." It's easy to wish that whatever you have were different. If you have a VW, you wish it were a Porsche. If you have someone who is strong and powerful, you wish he were sensitive and open. If you have someone who is fun and playful, you wish she were more serious and focused. The easy part is to hope and wish that whatever you have would be different. The challenging part is to let things and people be as they are. If they aren't O.K. with you then let them go; don't keep them around making them wrong because they aren't some other way.

DON'T
THINK,
DO!
■

There is a distinct difference between thinking and doing. *Thinking* is sitting around trying to figure out what to do. It is trying to do the right thing, and avoiding making a mistake. It is when you are solidly locked in your head. *Doing* is initiating action. Doing means jumping in and choosing something, anything, but taking action and moving from thinking to doing. So often we are afraid of doing the wrong thing that we stew and mull it over, believing that the more thinking we do the more sure we will be of the action taken. We feel that we are hedging our bets if we really think something through, but in reality it is more like a cat playing with a half-dead mouse: we poke it this way, then that way, and then jump on it, then crouch down, then spring up. Remember, it's not *what* you do but *that* you do something that matters.

USING
YOUR BODY
TO MANAGE
YOUR MIND
■

Think for a moment. Can you remember being down, depressed, or bummed out when you were vigorously physically active? Probably not. It is extremely difficult to have your mind beat up on you when you are jumping around. If you find yourself stuck in your head, getting grim, or closing down, do something physical. If you are in casual clothes, run or jump up and down. If you are in work clothes, take a brisk walk or swing your arms vigorously. If you are alone at home, put on music and dance around the living room. Don't get stuck in trying to figure our what the best activity is, just start moving around and it will come to you.

LETTING
THE CHILD
WITHIN
OUT TO PLAY
■

Raising my daughter is challenging to me, since I am not always sure how to be a good parent. I do try to notice every time she drives me crazy, and take a mini-inventory of my feelings. I often notice that I don't give myself permission to do what she is doing in my own life. The child within me rebels, and secretly says: "What about me? I never got to have my room a mess. How come you do? It's not fair!" I have made a list of all the things my daughter does that irk me, perturb me, or just plain drive me crazy. The following list belongs to the child within me who never got to be a kid:

1. Taking just a few bites of whatever is on my plate and leaving the rest
2. Wanting to eat only cookies, and letting myself do it
3. Being a mess
4. Dressing up
5. Leaving my room, the dishes, my desk, just about anywhere, a mess
6. Wearing my hair crazily, like in a pony tail in the middle of my head
7. Being silly
8. Dancing or singing around the house
9. Drawing, coloring, or painting with no objective in mind
10. Watching TV, lying around unproductively, or playing with dolls

When I become too compulsive or take life too seriously, I ask myself if maybe my child is feeling forgotten, deprived, or lost. If the answer is, "yes," then I need to set up some "kid time" for the child within me to play, and to just be able to be a kid.

KEEPING YOUR SENSE OF HUMOR
■

All too often you take yourself very seriously. Your life seems heavy and significant. Your problems and worries are traumatic and burdensome. Your life looks like the Book of Job. At times like these, it is infinitely helpful if you can lighten up. Find some humor in what is happening. See if you can't take some of the significance out of the heaviness. Have a friend on call to lighten and brighten your day. Norman Cousins said that laughter is the greatest healer, and he is right. Look for creative ways to tickle your funny bone.

A COMMITMENT
TO MAKING
MYSELF RIGHT,
NO MATTER WHAT
∎

Because of old patterns or old habits, it is easy to slip back into
self-criticism. Because of what someone says, or your reactions
to it, it is an old and familiar way of operating to invalidate
yourself for the way you are. You don't need to invalidate yourself—or anyone else for that matter—but you do need to back
yourself, no matter what. You need understanding, compassion, gentleness, and support, and you need it from YOU first
and foremost. After you have demonstrated that you can be
there for you, then you can allow another person to be there
as well, mirroring your relationship with yourself.

All of these are daily maintenance tools. It is critical that
you are equipped to handle emergencies. The next chapter is
about managing yourself under crisis.

EIGHT

ADDITIONAL
TOOLS
FOR
CRITICAL
MOMENTS

■

EMERGENCY
MEASURES

■

You now have the tools for daily maintenance, but what happens when you have a full-blown negattack? Vicious, vindictive, and venomous, a negattack can drive your self-esteem right down into the cellar. Consider the following techniques an emergency tool kit.

HELP!

■

It helps to know what to do, step-by-step, as if you were following a definite plan. If you don't know exactly what to do when a negattack hits unexpectedly, you may be in crisis before you know it. In order to design a procedure that will work for you,

you need to have a certain amount of self-knowledge. You need to know what immobilizes you, and what works to mobilize you. You need to know what works for you. You need to take action, and know how to reverse a downward spiral. The following are tools designed for critical moments rather than daily maintenance. When you are having a panic attack, a negattack, or when everything else fails, call on this list to pull yourself out of the ditch.

HOW TO CONDUCT AN ATTITUDE ADJUSTMENT
■

Perhaps you have noticed that there are moments when you are in a bad mood, or you're crabby, or you just feel grumpy. These are the times when you need an attitude adjustment. An attitude adjustment involves taking charge of a negaholic mind-set or behavior and reversing it. There are a variety of things that you can do, but first you must *want* to adjust your attitude. You must feel a need to change your state of being. If you do, here are some of the things you can do:

- Throw cold water on your face
- Go for a walk
- Listen to music that you love
- Lie down
- Take three deep breaths
- Scream into a pillow
- Get a hug from someone you love

USE
PANIC
CREATIVELY
■

Most addicted personalities get panicky at the thought of a negattack. The thought of having all the demons take over and start running the show is anxiety-producing to say the least. One way to counterbalance the negattack is to do the opposite of what most of us naturally do. When you imagine an attack coming on, you will most often put on the brakes, resist it, and try to back away from it. The resistance only creates persistence. You will become like a creature caught up in a tornado, sucked into the centripetal force of the velocity. The next time you anticipate a negattack coming on, instead of resisting it, go with it. Act it out, dramatize it, make it a gala theatrical demonstration of what is going on inside your head. Say the words, have your body move with the gestures and have fun making a grand physical display. Of course, you need to have a safe space to do it in, one where people will not judge you, where you can rant and rave with complete abandon. You don't want to try this at work, where people may think you are crazy, or in the grocery store, where they may have you locked up. The point is to have staked out those people and places which are safe for you, and where you can try on new behaviors and explore alternatives to your previous way of operating. Experiment with this, not as an answer but merely as an alternative to gray hair and ulcers.

PULVERIZING
A
PANIC ATTACK
■

Tina had to move. Her landlady had sold the house she was living in, and the date for the move had been set. Tina had carefully made plans to organize the move. She had figured out where she was going, where all of her things were going, and everything was ready. Three days before the move, she received a phone call from the woman she was moving in with saying that the woman had changed her mind and wanted to live alone, and would she please not move in. Tina had a full-blown panic attack. It sounded like this: "You idiot! Why did you plan to move in with her, you know how unpredictable she is. Now where are you going to go? You have screwed up everything!"

THIS
IS A JOB
FOR THE
GOOD FAIRY

■

Before Tina totally lost it, she called me and said, "Would you be the good fairy and tell me how everything that has happened to me is for the best. I've lost my perspective and the demons have taken over."

I, of course, agreed. Tina was at a loss about what to do. I suggested that she "listen for a message."

She complained that she had screwed everything up. I assured her that it was much better to know now how her new roommate felt *before* she moved in with her, rather than after the fact.

I emphasized, "If you don't know now, then you might have to go through the inconvenience of moving twice." Tina was still upset with her friend's inflexibility because of the limited time involved.

I urged her to consider the situation as a benefit, one which would save her wear and tear. "Finding out the truth later would only compound the situation," I said casually.

But Tina kept insisting, "I'll be out on the street, with nowhere to go."

I reminded her, "Look, things have always worked out in the past. When were you last on the street? Trust that things will work out. Put everything in God's hands; call everyone you know; ask who knows of a place where you can stay for a month. Then just wait and see what turns up."

And so the dialogue went, until Tina started hearing what the good fairy was saying to her, and the panic attack subsided. The function of the good fairy is to change the perspective and focus on the positive. See if there isn't someone in your life who could function as the good fairy. When you start to have a panic attack, you can send up a good fairy flare.

DESIGNING
YOUR
OWN
FIRE DRILL
■

When you were a child in school, you probably had fire drills to ensure that in the event of a real fire everyone would know exactly what to do. The fire drill was rehearsed so that all the children followed the procedure automatically, without thinking and without panicking. In my school, when the fire alarm sounded we immediately put down everything in our hands, stood up and silently formed a single line. We then calmly followed the head of the line, not running, but moving as swiftly as possible. I remember our fire drills to this day. If I heard the fire alarm I would respond as mechanically as Pavlov's dog, putting down everything I was holding, standing up, forming a single line, and filing out of the building in silence. A fire drill is very important to a negaholic. It is a procedure that you follow without thinking when you get a signal that you are in danger. You custom design it for yourself, and you rehearse it over and over so that it is drilled into your memory system when there is no emergency, so that when the alarm does go off, you respond automatically. For example, if you feel a negattack coming on, you might do one of the following:

- BREATHE. The first sign of an attack is arrested
  breathing. It may sound elementary, but taking

three deep breaths from your diaphragm can stop the machinery for an instant and give you a chance to get a hold of yourself. You may want to put a sign up in various strategic places—on your bathroom mirror, on the refrigerator, on the wall above your desk, on the dashboard of your car—to remind you to stop, breathe, and suspend the attack. BREATHE!

- START MOVING. Take a walk around the office, around the block, around your house; jump up and down in place; if jumping is too vigorous, march in place; if the environment can support it and you won't hurt yourself, stand on your head. Movement is critical to getting out of your head. After all, that is where negaholic attacks happen. So get into your body in order to get out of your head.

- MIRROR-SELF TALK. Coach yourself in the mirror. Carry one with you at all times. Your fire-drill buzzword may be *mirror*. Get me to a mirror! When you get to a mirror, you say kind, endearing words to yourself. "Hi, honey, it's O.K., you're doing the best you can. I understand, and I know what you're going through. I won't leave you, you can count on me, we'll get through this one together."

- IF YOU LIKE TO WRITE THINGS DOWN, then the buzzword might be *paper*. Use a pad of paper or your journal and let everything in your head flow out onto the piece of paper. Don't be concerned about making sense, or being organized. Just write down whatever is on your mind. You can look at it later, but for the moment just get it out of you.

- IF YOU LIKE TO TALK, then you may want to reach out. Reaching out takes two forms: face to face and over the phone. You may want to set up an agreement with a friend whereby you can have that person be your fire-drill buddy so you can call him/her when you feel a negattack coming on. You might even be able to use your answering machine if your friend is not available.

DO
IT RIGHT
■

One thing to watch for is trying to figure out the right way to do your fire drill. There *is* no right way. There is only *your way*, and your way is whatever works for you. Don't force yourself to design your fire drill in any way that is not easy and natural for you. Remember, a fire drill is automatic, and requires no effort. Your fire drill needs to be automatic, effortless, and mindless. The purpose of a fire drill is to get you to react automatically so that you can get yourself out of a potentially dangerous situation swiftly and efficiently and without thinking. This can be a fun exercise, especially if you take into consideration the way you work and what works for you.

These are the steps to designing an effective fire drill:

- First make a list of the situations, people, and environments in which you most often have negattacks.
- Then list "cues" which could snap you out of present time (or whatever time frame you have slipped into) and alert you that it is time to do something different.
- Choose one cue, and list four action steps you could take after receiving the cue. In school, it was stop, put everything down, form a single line in silence, and exit the building. Your fire drill must be that simple. You need to be able to receive the cue, and automatically respond with

four simple actions to get you out of potential
danger.

Ollie was highly reactive. He was afraid of his panic attacks.
He and I collaborated on a four-step fire drill, which he could
use whenever he felt panicky. He told me that the ring he wore
was very special to him and he wanted it to be part of the fire
drill. I thought this was a great beginning, and asked, "How
do you want to use the ring?"

"I want to think the word 'ring,' then I want to touch the
ring with the fingers of my other hand. Then I want to breathe.
Lastly, I want to recite my name, the date, time, and the place
where I am at that moment to remind myself who and where
I am. This procedure will enable me to get into the present
moment so that I can choose whether or not I want to get upset."

In the early stages of the negaholic recovery process, it is
important to know how to deal with negattacks; they will diminish, but in the beginning they will still be present.

ONE
DAY
AT A TIME
■

"One day at a time" is a phrase used by Alcoholics Anonymous
and is enormously valuable to any addicted personality. The
addicted personality tends to view situations as a continuum
with no mileposts, no beginning, and no end. The phrase "one
day at a time" puts things into perspective so that you focus
on today, not the rest of your life, or the next ten years, but
just getting through one day: today. Whether it means going
without a cigarette, without sugar, or without beating yourself
up, the commitment is not forever, for a year, or even for three
months, it is for today. Making a commitment for forever is
frightening. If you have an addictive personality, it is difficult
to trust yourself to do or not to do something "forever." We
have little idea of what forever means.

Most people can imagine making and keeping a commitment for one day: today. You have a sense of what a day means,
and for one day you can trust yourself to do what you have
committed to. There are times, however, when one day seems
like too much to confront. At those times, commit yourself to
whatever works. Commit yourself to one hour at a time, and
then check in after one hour and see how you are doing. Then
renew your commitment for the next hour and congratulate
yourself for keeping your commitment for the last hour, and
so on.

THE
PRACTICAL
USE OF
PRAYER
■

Prayer does not have to be something that is reserved for the
clergy, the very holy, or people who are devoting their lives to
a religious sect. Prayer in the simplest of terms is having a
talk with an entity who has a broader perspective than you
have and can possibly affect changes over which you have little
or no power. The two most basic forms of prayer are asking for
something and thanking for something. Asking for something
is simply making a request: "Could I please have some water,"
"I would like to go to the beach." Praying is reaching out and
asking for what you want. "Please, God, I would like to get
through this day." "God, could you help me stop beating myself
up, please!" "God, I'd really like to have a new client within
the next thirty days, if it is the right thing in the grand scheme
of things."

The other side of prayer is thanking. You must remember
to say thank you whenever you get what you want, that is if
you want to have more of your wishes granted. So when you
get the new client that you requested, you say, "Thanks so
much for hearing my prayers and bringing me a new client."

THE
PITFALLS
OF PRAYER
■

There are two major pitfalls for which you must watch. The first is turning everything over to God and sitting back and doing nothing yourself to bring about the desired results. The second pitfall is that, after receiving something which you requested, you think you did it all by yourself with no help from the outside. If you prayed, you need to acknowledge that you did so. If you take all the credit yourself, then you invalidate the fact that you had your prayers answered or that God intervened and helped you in the process. You need to watch out for these two extremes: helplessness and taking credit. Remember, you don't even have to believe in a God in order to pray.

COUNTING
YOUR
BLESSINGS
■

Like all addicted negaholics, we tend to focus on the negative. There is a childhood game which shows three addition problems:

$$\begin{array}{ccc} 6 & 8 & 9 \\ +4 & +5 & +7 \\ \hline 10 & 12 & 16 \end{array}$$

When you look at the three sets of addition problems above, what do you see? Now answer honestly. Do you see two that are accurate and one that is inaccurate? Do you see one that is just one off? Or do you see the way most of us are trained to see, "There's one that's WRONG!" Most of us look at those three addition problems and see only one thing: the one that is wrong. We don't even notice the two that are correct. We only notice that which is wrong. Just as when you read the newspapers, what is the focus? You read about bombings, murders, rapes, droughts, assassinations, fires, wars; about exposing graft, corruption, dishonesty, immorality, and character flaws in our leaders. For the most part, our society focuses on what is negative, and we are subconsciously trained to think this way. We discount the positive and dwell on the negative.

In order to change this mind-set, you have to behave like a salmon swimming upstream, you have to go against the current. This applies not only to your world focus, but also to your focus in your own life. It pertains to the way you focus on your relationship with yourself as well as your relationship to those around you. So often we take things for granted. The most obvious is our health. We take for granted the fact that we are healthy. You start to appreciate your health when you no longer have it.

Joan, a client and friend, had a bad case of flu that she couldn't get rid of. It stayed with her for over three months, and she felt just awful. She was really grateful when it finally went away. Not only do we take our health for granted, but we take harmony with our primary relationships for granted. We look at getting what we want as a matter of course. When our life goes smoothly, we take it in our stride. The more we take the little benefits and gifts that life has to offer for granted, the more astonished we are when things don't go our way.

MANEUVERING OUT OF THE MUCK AND MIRE

Nancy was having particular difficulties with her primary relationship. She and Robert were picking on each other and fighting about the tiniest things. She was clearly distressed. I

asked her if there was anything to be grateful for, and she
replied sadly, "I don't think so." The problems she was experiencing in her relationship had eclipsed everything else.

I pushed her to look and see if there wasn't just one thing
that she could be grateful for.

She thought for a moment, and said glumly, "I'm alive, I
guess I could be thankful for that."

I said, "That's a start, is there another?"

After some rooting around she started to name things that
she could be grateful for. First, her daughter was healthy,
happy, and in great shape. She was doing some of the best work
that she had ever done. Then, come to think of it, her car was
running well, her bills were paid, her hair looked good, and
she'd actually lost two pounds. She got started on a roll, and
began to snowball.

Her face started to change before my eyes, and I watched
her brighten and lighten up. She started to get excited and all
by herself (with just a little coaxing) pulled herself out of the
muck and mire and into the sunlight.

When you are feeling caught in the muck, make yourself
a "blessings" list. On this list you put everything you have to
be grateful for. You list the obvious, and especially those things
which you normally would take for granted. After you write
it, then you must read it over three times to let it sink in.

REACHING
OUT
TO OTHERS
■

As I have said before, it is so easy to lose your perspective. It
is easy to forget that other people have situations in their lives
which are similar to your own. The crashing blow to your ego
is that you are not alone; your problems may seem horrendous,
but they are not unique, and someone, somewhere, has probably been through all these things. This is disarming to most
of us, who think that our problems are the most significant,

the most serious, and should be kept as deep dark secrets. We think that no one would understand, and that we have the greatest sin ever.

In a long-term group training program which I was conducting, a woman in the group confessed her deepest darkest secret in order to stop feeling as if there was something wrong with her. She felt she carried a black spot, which sullied her and made her less than everyone else. She bared her soul to the group and with enormous shame told them that she had contracted a vaginal virus. She did this with great reluctance, and her confession took her a long time to get out. The moment she told her secret, eighty percent of the group said, "Oh, I've had that, too." She was shocked, relieved, and pleased that she wasn't alone, pleased that the group understood. She was *not* Hester Prynne with the scarlet A on her chest. Knowing that she was not alone brought relief and comfort. Usually women have an easier time sharing their problems, secrets, and concerns than men do. This is an area where men's support groups can really help men come out of isolation and gain perspective and help from one another.

The truth of the matter is that the more you reach out to others to gain perspective, validity, or support, the more you feel "normal." It is important to feel "normal." The more "different" you feel, the more you feel alienation, distance, and separation. The more distance and alienation you feel, the greater a negaholic you can become. The reason is that you draw into yourself, with only you to talk to, and lo and behold! the voices have taken over. Before you know it you have a reign of terror on your hands.

OVERCOMING EMBARRASSMENT

Reaching out to others is often embarrassing. The reason it is embarrassing is because we think we are supposed to be perfect, know all the answers, not need anyone, and be able to handle doing everything for ourselves. To admit that we are not perfect, that we don't have all the answers, and that we may need someone outside ourselves to help is embarrassing.

THE
NEED TO
BE PERFECT
■

I was in Des Moines conducting a workshop, and one of the participants bravely admitted to me: "We are nice people who don't have many problems, and what's more, we're supposed to be perfect. We're busy upholding that image of perfect people. So we don't want you or even each other to know that we don't have it all together."

I thought that that brave and honest statement was very telling, not only about Des Moines, but about people in general. How many of us have the unrealistic expectation that we are supposed to be perfect, to do everything perfectly the first time, and to have no problems? How cruel of us to inflict this pressure on ourselves.

MURMUR
A MANTRA
■

When you find yourself in the familiar perfectionist pattern, choose a slogan, or murmur a mantra to remind you that it can be different. Here are some examples of ones to choose:

- "You only learn from making mistakes. You have to do something in order to make a mistake, in order to learn."
- "Everything is practice."
- "People who don't make mistakes don't make anything."
- "I do have a choice. I can choose to not be perfectionistic."

USING
POSITIVE TRIGGERS
AS A TAP
ON THE SHOULDER

Just like murmuring mantras, having "pet phrases," which you can call forth at moments of need, really helps. These pet phrases act as positive triggers and serve as a tap on the shoulder. Their purpose is to remind you that you don't have to handle this situation in the same way that you have always handled it before. You have the right, the ability, and the power to change your behavior if you want to. We so often forget this, that we need reminders. We think that either we don't have the right, or we're unable, or we don't possess the power to change our behavior.

Some examples of pet phrases are:

- This is a pattern.
- You have the power to choose.
- You don't have to go crazy.
- How could you do this quite differently?
- This situation is temporary, it will pass.
- Hang in there, in a couple of hours all will be different.

Choose one of the above or make up your own. Write it down and stick it in strategic places around your house, office, or in your car. Use it whenever you need a reminder that you are in charge, that you can run your life the way you choose.

THE
POWER
OF CHOICE

You forget how much power you really have. When you choose something, you exercise your ability and your power to determine what is going to happen. You demonstrate that you know what needs to happen, that you are willing to say what needs to happen, and that you are willing to be responsible for the consequences resulting from your choice. When you choose, you silence the nay-sayer and move into the land of certainty. You take action with direction and conviction. When you remain indecisive, you inhibit your innate knowingness, your ability to cause things to happen. It is very important to remember that you have the power to choose.

HOW TO
GET THE FUN BACK
IN LIFE WHEN
YOU'VE LOST IT
■

There seem to be times for all of us when life is just no fun. Work is a drag, the routine seems to be getting to you, and your relationship is about who is taking out the garbage. Nothing is exciting, or fun. Everything seems grim and dreary. At these times the best thing you can do is something really zany. When you do something zany and crazy, you jostle all the molecules, and change the energy. Changing the energy is critical, since the routine has locked you into a pattern which is sedentary, boring, and predictable. Break out, take a walk on the wild side, and do something different, something just a little risky. Play, do something you normally don't do, or be downright outrageous! Now I'm not suggesting that you do anything illegal, immoral, or fattening, but I am hinting that you might just cut loose to change the energy.

MAYBE
IT'S BEHIND
THE MAYONNAISE?
■

Lucy was always entertaining to listen to. One day she came into my office and said, "My objective for this session is to find out what I am doing when I wander aimlessly around the kitchen." I wasn't really sure what she was talking about, and asked for an explanation.

She said, "It happened just the other night. I went into the kitchen and opened the fridge, looked around, then closed it. Then I went to the cupboard, opened it, looked around, and then closed it. Then I went to the bread bin, rooted around, and then closed it. And then I went back to the fridge, opened the door, and thought to myself, 'It must be here. I know it must be here!' I stood there looking into this array of food thinking, 'Is it behind the mayonnaise? Or maybe it's hiding behind the milk? Perhaps it's in one of the drawers?' I found myself looking for something, and the truth of the matter is that I wasn't even hungry. I was looking for something to fill a hole."

Lucy wanted to be able to stop acting this way, and to know what was at the root of her behavior.

When you find yourself on automatic, stop, if you can, and ask yourself what you are feeling. See if you can get in touch with it, instead of automatically trying to fill up the feeling.

WHAT DO YOU DO IF YOU GET NO MESSAGES AT ALL?

Do not panic. Stop what you are doing, sit quietly, and ask for a message. After asking for a message, listen. It's as if you were talking into a telephone and then stopped and waited for a response. You need to listen for the message to come. Messages come in a variety of ways. They come to you through direct knowing, through other people telling you things, through books and assorted reading material, in just about any form imaginable.

Messages are fundamental to the negaholic recovery process. Not only do they encourage you to trust your intuition and look at the big picture, but they also remind you that if you are willing to listen, your life can be guided by a wise, benevolent force. The next chapter will give you more information about messages.

NINE

LISTEN TO YOUR INNER WISDOM

■

We all have an inner sense of rightness. Rightness about people, about places, about when it's time to do something, about when it's time to stop or avoid doing something. You've no doubt heard of, "a time to plant, and a time to pluck up that which is planted; . . . a time to gather stones together." Well, there is more to this than simply following the seasons, watching the cycles of the moon, or the position of the stars. Some people call it a sixth sense. Others call it female intuition, although it is my experience that men have it just as much as women, if they choose to tune into it. It has been called intuition, inner knowing, inner guide, instinct, gut-level sense, higher self, and connection with the infinite, but the real truth of the matter is that if and when we are really honest about our inner workings, there is a lot more going on than most of us usually admit.

SPIRITUAL
DNA,
THE INNER
GUIDE

I like to call it spiritual DNA. I feel that we are born with an inner wisdom, which resides deep within us and transmits messages about the choices that are right for us. If you listen carefully, you can tune into this frequency, which transmits information all the time. It never stops, but we have the choice to tune in and listen or tune out. Your radio, for instance, is always transmitting, but you may not always choose to listen to it. You may turn the volume down low, or completely off. Regardless of the volume level, the radio keeps on transmitting whether you are listening or not.

This spiritual DNA sends you messages about everything: when you need to exercise, when you need to rest, when you need to be with people, and when you need to be alone. The messages come from within and transmit cues that tell you what your self needs for its well-being moment to moment. The problem is that the messages usually don't coincide with *your* idea of what you are supposed to be doing at the moment.

For instance, in the middle of writing a paper, you might get a message to call a friend across the country. You probably don't know why you are getting this message at this particular moment, but you have a choice: to argue with the message or to act on it. If you argue with it, which is what most people do, you will think: This isn't the best time to call, I'm too busy right now, she's probably not there, I'm too tired, I don't feel like it, I'll do it later. More often than not, when you listen to the message, your friend will be there, possibly answer the phone, and she may even say, "I was just thinking of *you*, how strange of you to call right now."

It will tell you when you need to take a break, when you need to lie down, to have some quiet time, to take a walk, or go to a certain restaurant. If you listen closely, you will have clear clues about when to travel, when to stay home, when to change jobs, when to get out of a relationship, and when to hang in there.

Messages give you all kinds of information all the time. It seems rather disconcerting when you've planned to do something and the message has other ideas. You plan to take a nap and the message says to get up and write something down so you won't forget. You plan to go to lunch and the message says to stop and go to the restroom. You plan to read a book and the message says to take a walk. If you are tuned in to the messages you may start to wonder who is in charge, you or the messages.

There are two main problems about listening to the messages. When your mind is chattering at you, you literally can't hear them. The messages are quiet whispers, and the mind chatter by comparison seems to come through loud megaphones, drowning out those subtle messages. It's as if you were playing Pachelbel's Canon in D on the volume level of a three on the stereo, and your neighbor, in the next room put on John Philip Sousa at the volume level of ten. It's simply hard to hear with the mind chatter jabbering away.

The second problem is that when you do hear the messages, you frequently don't listen to what they are telling you. Since they sound so bizarre and absurd, you dismiss them as if they were gnats flying around your head. Instead of listening, you discount, discredit, disown, ignore, and blatantly disregard these subtle and repetitious messages which are transmitted all the time. If you are out of touch with your feelings, and you discredit your messages, it is normal for you to end up in a place called, "I don't know." What is required is that you be able to hear, listen, allow, trust, and even act on the messages for guidance about your life.

You get messages about everything. You even get messages about what to eat and how much to eat. Some messages come in the form of feelings, and others are like sounds or sensations.

LISTEN
FOR THE
BONG

■

Your body tells you when you've had enough to eat. The problem is that most people don't like the body's sense of timing or its capacity. Try this exercise the next time you sit down to eat a meal. First of all choose what you and your body want to eat. Actually have a consultation with your body. Ask your body what it wants to eat. Then listen for the answer. When you get the answer, don't judge it or criticize it, just listen and accept what it says. Then prepare your meal. If you don't have what was agreed upon in the house, then go buy it, or go to a restaurant and order your stomach's desire.

When the plate of food is in front of you, take a deep breath before you begin to eat. After you take a bite, put your fork down and chew your food thoroughly. Make sure that you breathe while you are chewing and that you swallow before you pick up your fork or knife. Do this every time you take another mouthful. While you are chewing your food, don't cut and prepare the next bite, butter your bread, or sip your beverage. Focus your attention on chewing, breathing, and experiencing your food.

During this process, listen for the *Bong*. The *Bong* is a feeling in your abdominal area which lets you know that you have had enough food. It is a subtle message from your digestive tract which says, "That's enough, thank you." It is a feeling which you may have never heard before, but it is real, and if you listen, you will hear it. Often people complain to me: "I have a premature *Bong!*" They don't like hearing their *Bong* so soon. They say they're disappointed that they have to stop eating too early. They are upset that they have to stop the pleasant process of eating because of this dumb *Bong*.

I remind them that they can save the food and eat it later. If they are in a restaurant, they can have it wrapped up to take home to some needy pet if they don't want to admit the truth.

You have to believe that this is not your last chance to eat, or that you only have thirty minutes to pack in all the pleasure you can get.

Use the *Bong* exercise to listen to your inner digestive guide. Trust it, honor it, and choose when and how much you want to eat.

A
MESSAGE
TO
MOVE

Let me give you another example. Simon first came to California in 1970. He was on vacation in San Francisco, a place he had always wanted to go, and while he was there, he had a very strong feeling that someday he would leave New York and be living in Northern California. He didn't know when, or under what circumstances, but he knew that someday he would live in the Bay Area.

At first this was disconcerting to him. He stewed about it, wondered, and tried to figure out all the specifics: When would it be? What would he be doing? Where would he live? How would he support himself? Of course he didn't have any answers, so it was pointless to ponder these questions. But that didn't matter; he was confused and wanted to know what was going to happen.

His inner sense was telegraphing something precognitive. In other words, he knew something through direct knowing. He wouldn't have the data for explaining why he had to do this, but the intuition was very clear to him. He knew something that was going to happen in the future before he ever had the right to know the information.

Years passed and he became involved in projects and activities and forgot about his California message. One day when he was living in New York, he received a phone call from a friend and colleague who invited him to come to San Francisco. At the time he was in transition, eagerly anticipating what was going to be the next step in his life. He accepted the invitation to come to San Francisco and without making a connection between his 1970 message and this adventure, he set off. When he arrived, he stayed with old friends whom he had known from the East, and he became involved in the San Francisco lifestyle.

About the third day it hit him: This was the fulfillment of the message that he had received four years ago. He knew that there was a rightness to being in San Francisco at this time, even though he couldn't explain it. He knew the day would come and here it was. He knew about this before he could know. It felt almost like déjà-vu. He would discover that there were lessons for him to learn, and an important phase of his development would unfold here. San Francisco was the right place for this chapter of his life.

THE
MESSAGE
IS THE MEDIUM:
IT GETS YOU UNSTUCK

Diana was a window dresser who styled department-store windows. She was having difficulty getting a job. In our session together, I asked her innocently, "Diana, is there anything that you'd rather be doing beside window dressing?"

She said, "What do you mean?"

I said, "Well, usually when people are clear about what they want they tend to get it. If they don't get what they want then there is usually something in the way. Either they don't believe that they can have what they want, they are afraid to get everything that they want, or they may be clinging to what they used to do, what they should be doing, and not what they truly want to do right now—in other words, their heart's desire."

She thought about it for ten seconds, and said, "You want to know what I really want to do?"

I said "Yes, if it isn't window dressing, what *do* you want to do? Or where would you rather be?"

She burst out as if a flood of water had broken down the gates: "Well, I'd rather be in Paris, of course. Wouldn't everybody?"

I responded, "Actually, no, but that's irrelevant; is that where you'd rather be?"

"My God, I'd like to be in Paris more than breathe, but I couldn't possibly. I mean I have a house, and a child, and responsibilities. I couldn't possibly."

Throughout our conversation I reminded her that the path she was on was riddled with struggle, force, and effort. I asked her if there was any relationship between where she was in her life and how she felt about going to Paris.

She finally told the truth and said that she had been dressing windows for fifteen years and she didn't want to do it anymore. She said that she had been denying the message to go to Paris for the longest time. She was impassioned with Paris, and it was the only thing that mattered to her.

I told her that it didn't matter to me if she lived in the States or in Europe, and that she herself was the only one who really cared about where she lived. She pondered and vacillated several times, and finally resolved that she would take the risk and go for her dream: to live in Paris. Within twenty-four hours she had rented her house; in ten days she had dealt with her responsibilities, scooped up her daughter, and left for Paris.

I received a postcard a month later saying, "Thank you for encouraging me to listen to what I was unwilling to hear. I love it here. I've never been happier. I am in the right place, all will come together now. Bless you! Love, Diana."

Messages are like that. They are irrational, illogical, and unreasonable. They make no sense, but they feel right. Listening to the messages is like operating from a different reality. When you live life listening to the messages, you are separating yourself from the confused mainstream. Messages don't fit into the scientific, rational, analytic system. When you live life in touch with your higher self, listening to those subtle messages, some people may think you've lost your grip on reality. It's quite different from anything they taught us in school.

Your mind will have a tough time with messages because of all the questions that remain unanswered. Questions like, "How do you know the difference between a message and your mind chatter? What is the difference between a message and just being lazy? How do you know when you are just being self-indulgent? Can't listening to your messages get you into trouble?" Of course there are responses to these questions, but what the questions are really saying is: "This is so alien from anything I've ever been taught that it frightens me. I'm scared of these notions because there isn't anything to hold on to. Given my upbringing, it seems far out and weird."

GO
STAND ON
THE CORNER!
■

Buzz went to business school at a prestigious Eastern University, was very traditional, and upheld his parents' values. Buzz was visiting Boston with his wife and two other couples. They all agreed to meet at a restaurant for dinner, and because of the size of the group they decided to take two cars. Buzz and his wife got to the restaurant first and waited for the others to join them. They waited for what seemed the longest time. When the wine came, Buzz got a message to "go stand on the corner," which he rationalized by saying to himself, "Why should I stand on the corner when everybody knows where we agreed to meet? Besides, it's February and it's cold and snowy outside. They'll be here any minute."

After the salad arrived, he heard the inner message again, only this time it was clearer and louder. "Go stand on the corner." By this time he was feeling edgy, but remained stubborn and firm and held his ground.

He argued with the message. "Look, they know where we're meeting. They are intelligent people. I am enjoying being with my wife, keeping warm, drinking my wine, and listening to the music."

When the waiter returned for the third time to take their order, he heard inside his head: "GO STAND ON THE CORNER!" loud and clear. He had fought and was resistant but now he thought, "Enough already!" He turned to his wife resignedly and said, "I'm going to stand on the corner."

She asked why. He said, "Don't ask, I'll be right back."

Buzz walked through the restaurant muttering to himself and feeling rather silly. No sooner had he gotten to the corner but up drove the car with the two couples. He was amazed, but so were they. They asked him why he was standing on the corner, and he said that he would explain everything inside over a glass of wine. The two other couples parked their car and when all six were seated the tale was unraveled.

The others had gone to another restaurant with the same name, couldn't find Buzz and his wife, and had almost given up the idea of having dinner with them when all of a sudden, as they were driving around Boston, there was Buzz standing on the corner. They all had a good laugh, and Buzz secretly questioned where the notion came from to stand on the corner in the first place.

There is a strange and inexplicable feeling of rightness with choices that come from inside yourself. You don't know why you are saying something, or why you are doing something, but you know on some level it's right. Messages are the clues in the scavenger hunt of life. They rarely make sense. They just tell you where to go or what to do, and you're supposed to trust the message and follow it if you want to win the prize. Whoever said that life was a scavenger hunt?

Messages take many different forms. They can come in the form of inner directives, as Buzz's did. They can come in the form of several friends suggesting that you do something. Messages can be phone calls, letters, books, periodicals, literally any way that you can receive information. The tip-off is that if it is a message, it doesn't go away. It is recurring and incessant. In addition, after three repetitions of the same message, it's a good idea to stop, look, and listen.

THE
LORD
WILL SAVE ME!
■

There is a story about a very religious man who lived alone in his house. He prayed every day, and felt that if anything terrible ever happened the Lord would be there and take care of him.

One day it started to rain. It rained and rained and began to flood.

Some people came running by, wading through the water, saying, "Come with us to safety, hurry!"

His reply was, "The Lord will save me."

The water level rose and a car drove by, barely making it through the deep water, and the people inside said, "Get in, we have enough room, we'll take you to a safe place. But hurry, there is not much time."

His response was, "Thank you kindly, but the Lord will save me. The Lord will save me!"

The water level rose so high that he had to go up to the second story of his house to stay dry.

A boat came by, and the people said, "We'll throw you a life preserver, grab on and we'll bring you on board."

His reply was, "Bless you all, but the Lord will save me. Go your way. I'm awaiting on the Lord."

Finally he was standing on the roof of the house with the water level rising fast. A helicopter passed overhead and the pilot shouted down, "I'll toss you a line and we'll hoist you up."

Predictably he said, "The Lord will save me. Any minute, you watch, the Lord will do something and I will be saved!"

Within minutes the water level rose and covered his whole body. Shortly thereafter he drowned. He ended up in heaven.

When the Lord was reviewing the list of new arrivals, He said to the man, "You're not supposed to be here! It's not your time. What are you doing here?"

The man said to the Lord. "I believed in You. I believed that You would save me. I waited and waited, and You never came. What happened?" The Lord replied, "I sent you a car, a boat, and a helicopter. What more do you want?"

The point is that messages come in many forms, and you need to be tuned in to pick up on the clues. The clues are always there, but sometimes you get locked in to how the message is *supposed* to look. You are busy looking for burning bushes, or for ducks to drop out of the sky, when in fact the message may be right in front of your face every day of your life and you are blind to it because you're looking for a totally different form than what you see. You can't get attached to things looking the way you think they should look, because in actuality they often don't fit your mental pictures of how they should look.

MESSAGES
WILL
KNOCK YOU DOWN
IF THEY HAVE TO

George was under considerable stress. He was moving to another apartment, which was disorienting. He was having difficulties with the woman in his life, which was causing him some discomfort, and he was working too hard. He kept getting the message to lie down and take it easy. He blatantly ignored the messages and just pushed harder. The messages came in many forms: in the form of his aching muscles, his wife, his fatigue level, and daily headaches. He simply would not slow down. He only pushed harder. One day he bent down to lift a box, and his back seized up. He went into spasm and couldn't move. He was temporarily paralyzed. In a few hours an ambulance came and took him to the hospital where he was put under medication until the spasms subsided. As George lay in his hospital bed reviewing the immediate past, he realized how much he had been ignoring the clues. At this point, George no longer had a choice. Whether he wanted to or not, he finally had to lie down. He resolved for the future to listen to the messages before they knocked him flat.

MESSAGES
COME
THROUGH
LOUD AND CLEAR

■

While meeting with her partner, Alex, Sally asked that all calls be diverted to her secretary, who received at least twenty calls. Once and only once during the meeting, Sally got the "message" to pick up the phone herself. That call was precisely the one that she needed to take. It was from Max, her third partner in the business, whom she had been trying to track down for two days. She couldn't explain the feeling she had to take this call.

"I just had a strong, clear urge to pick up the phone after one ring," she said to Alex.

MESSAGES
AREN'T
ALWAYS WHAT
THEY APPEAR

■

Joe kept having the urge to move to Washington. It was driving him crazy. He kept saying, "I don't have a job in Washington, or a place to live, and really what am I going to do? Move to Washington and hang out?"

He was upset by this nagging message. It was recurring and driving him crazy.

One day he was walking down the street and a piece of a torn novel was blown up against his legs. He bent down and picked it up, and the first line said, "Libbie was puzzled. Of course she'd like the opportunity to go to Washington, but why was Cole making such a big deal of it?"

Joe nearly freaked out. "Yikes," he thought, "these messages are coming from all over."

When we met, he was still shaken by this strange occurrence. I asked him what he wanted to do about the message, his recurring feelings, and now the page from the novel. He admitted that the signs were a little much for him. He felt that he needed to go to Washington to at least check it out and see what was pulling him there. He figured that when he got there he would get another clue. It might just get clear.

Joe did go to Washington, and it was there that he met Pam. It was a fortuitous meeting, and they started planning their future together.

CREATIVE MESSAGES
■

Marion had never painted, and the only drawing class she ever attended turned out to be a disaster. She found that the only thing she could draw was a cocktail glass with champagne bubbles coming out of it. She never thought that she was artistic, and her art teachers confirmed her suspicions.

Fifteen years later, after the drawing-class incident, in a city far, far away, she found herself in traffic school doodling on a notebook. She was becoming enmeshed in her lovely little doodles. As the days went by she found that she was drawn to doodle more and more. She went with it and allowed herself to doodle away.

The next urge she had was to add color to the doodles, to fill in the spaces with her favorite colors. The doodling and coloring progressed and developed. Before too long, she found herself in a paint store buying iridescent paints in her favorite aquas, peaches, and mint greens. The doodles, which had started on little squares of paper, had grown and grown. Now the little squares had grown into five-foot-square canvases.

Marion had her first gallery opening, and sold six of her paintings. She still couldn't draw, but her ability to use color and light were earning her a living as an artist.

Marion had a message to doodle, then to add color, and then to paint. The message never made sense to her, but they never really do. It didn't matter anyway; she was listening to her messages and loving her art.

THE MESSAGE CENTER GENERATES MAGIC
■

The message center is the generator of the sparks. The sparks are those little pieces of electricity which get you charged up, motivated, and raring to go. When you listen to the messages, the sparks come alive.

THE SUPPOSE-TO SHUFFLE
■

When we are children, we usually learn to behave. *Behave* means different things to different people, but most often it means to be considerate, responsible, appropriate, and polite. These are desirable things to learn. They not only make you a welcome guest, but they also make you a likable person. If you are considerate, responsible, appropriate, and polite, then you are socially acceptable; you are a desirable business partner and also a good friend. The problem is that some people get stuck in behaving in these four ways and start to live according to the "shoulds," the "suppose-tos," the "ought-tos," and leave themselves entirely out of the process. In other words, they live their lives for the approval and acceptance of others.

They behave in the way they are supposed to, and they are always appropriate, but they are behaving this way because it fulfills other people's expectations. When you behave the way you "should" behave, you tend to obscure the messages. When the "shoulds" run your life, there isn't a lot of fun. The subtle little messages get lost in the suppose-to shuffle.

The sparks disappear when the suppose-tos run the show.

USING
THE MESSAGE
GAME
AS A BLUDGEON
■

Some negaholics know about messages. Those who do can be dangerous, because they will use the message game against themselves. The process looks like this:

Negaholics receive messages which they can't or won't accept. In other words, the messages are too outrageous, too expensive, or too risky. The message is rejected as unacceptable. When the message is unacceptable, it is discarded. The negaholic then proceeds to criticize himself for getting this absurd message, for not listening to the message, or for not acting on the message. (You can always find a good reason to beat yourself up.) The cycle is continued whereby the negaholic is beaten for listening or for not listening, for not trusting, for not taking action, and so on. And this is how negaholics can turn the message game into more creative ways to flagellate themselves. When you don't trust your messages, and you beat yourself for whatever messages you do and don't get, then it stands to reason that you can't possibly know what you want.

BATTLING
THE
MESSAGES

Since, as I said before, messages are irrational, illogical, and unreasonable, they never make sense. If you are an analytical, rational, left-brain type, messages will drive you crazy. You will actually do battle with them.

For example, Emily was moving and she got the message to live alone. This felt really right to her, but when Herb, her lover, found out about this, he said, "I'll hear none of it. You'll live with me. That's all there is to it." On one level she felt taken care of and loved, but on another, she felt strange and unsettled inside. She couldn't figure out why she felt so uneasy, but she knew something wasn't right.

Instead of telling the truth about her feelings, she kept judging herself for how she felt. She was angry that she couldn't make everything work at Herb's house. She was judging herself as picky, uptight, or neurotic. She told herself that she wouldn't be happy anywhere, that she should be grateful to Herb and stay put. She was afraid of hurting Herb's feelings by telling him that she didn't want to live with him. She felt guilty for not wanting to be with him, since he was being so sweet and considerate. Herb actually offered to move out and let her have his place for a week if it would help matters. She only felt more guilt. She thought she should stay just to be nice to Herb; after all, he had been so accommodating and considerate to her. But on the other hand, she couldn't sleep or rest easy, since she didn't know where she belonged.

Emily was in mental torment. She wouldn't heed her message to live alone, nor could she make things work out with Herb. Whichever way she turned, she felt that the great guillotine in the sky was going to come down and chop off her head for doing the wrong thing. She was fearful, and panicky, and beating herself all the time.

In our session together, I asked her when was the last time she had written an acknowledgment list. She told me it had been weeks. I asked her to please write one so that she could see what she had accomplished recently. Then I asked her, if she could live anywhere at all, where she would want to live. She said it would be in a loft with lots of light and space and air. She wanted it to be all white like a cloud, and to be peaceful and calm. She wanted to feel at peace more than anything else. I asked her if she believed that this was possible, and she said "yes." We then had a session to induce whatever message was lurking within to come to the surface.

The more she gave herself permission to be herself, to be wherever she was, to feel whatever she felt, and to listen to her messages, the more peaceful and calm she became. The more she listened to her messages and trusted what she felt and heard within, the less she was tempted to beat herself up. The choice for Emily was between whether she wanted to be angry at herself for her thoughts, her feelings, her messages, or whether she wanted to be gentle with herself and honor her thoughts, feelings, and messages as her truth.

Some people think that if they follow their messages, then surely there will be a happy ending. There may very well be a happy ending in your life, but the real point of listening to the messages is to learn the lessons that you need to learn, so that you can get to where you want to go. Learning lessons allows you to fulfill your purpose in life. Messages also encourage you to live your life fully and joyfully.

The main criticism I get from people about living the message game is an onslaught of "yeah-buts" like: "Yeah-but, *you* don't have to go to a job every day that you hate," "Yeah-but, what if I got a message to leave my husband? I have responsibilities, do you suggest that I just leave?", "Yeah-but, you don't have it nearly as bad as I do, I can't just listen to my messages. What if I got a message to stay home. What do you suggest I do, quit my job?"

Now I am *not* suggesting that you behave irresponsibly, or abandon those people, responsibilities, and duties which are currently in your life. Far from it, if you behaved in an irresponsible manner, you would beat yourself mercilessly, and then we would be right back where we started. It would be a pointless exercise. Living up to your standards, being the person you know you truly are, and being gentle with yourself while you learn your lessons, are the fundamentals that will get you started on the road to recovery.

The next chapter will help you launch yourself into your new life.

TEN

THE
ROAD
TO
RECOVERY

■

The road to recovery is, as they say in A.A., one step at a time, one day at a time, even one moment at a time. You need to be patient, compassionate, and understanding with yourself, since changing old patterns doesn't happen overnight. You need to get off your back, stop driving yourself, and give yourself permission to be human. You need to be kind, considerate, and gentle with yourself. You need to do unto yourself as you do unto others!

You've seen in this book that negativity is a very common addiction, and that there *is* a way out of the negaholic trap. But even if you know all the techniques that can help you get out—even if you clearly understand where the negaholic syndrome is coming from—that knowledge will be of no use to you unless you utilize it. Unless you really want to take control of your negaholism, turn it around so that you get what you want and can refocus your energy in a positive way, knowing all the techniques we've discussed won't help you. *You have to want to control your negaholism!*

There are reasons and there are results. You can either have the result—getting what you want—or you can have the reasons, explanations, and justifications as to why you *can't* have what you want. The choice is up to you.

POSITIVE SELF-REGARD
■

Liking yourself and being gentle with yourself is what this book has been about, thinking enough about yourself to allow yourself all the goodies in life; knowing you deserve all that is good and letting yourself have the pleasures, the treasures, and the leisures that make life worth living. You have to want your life to be wonderful. And you have to believe that it is possible to have it that way. Then you have to know that *you* can have it that way. You need to do what it takes. That means you must push through, let go, cause, accept, allow, feel, pray, listen to the messages—anything you need to do so that you can dissolve your negaholism and bring about your heart's desires.

SELF-TRUST
■

In addition to liking yourself, you need to trust your inner wisdom. Those subtle messages that come through and tap you on the shoulder are your link with your true path. Listen, trust what you hear, and as long as your message doesn't hurt yourself or anyone else, act on it. Remember, your messages are your inner spiritual DNA and your outer road map to finding and following your path.

RECRUITING
A
SUPPORT TEAM
■

If God had meant us to operate autonomously, he would have given each of us our own individual island. The reason why we have people all around us is so that we can learn to live together and support one another. Being self-consumed and caring only about your own needs and wants is shortsighted and isolationist. Caring only about others and forgetting about yourself is a recipe for resentment and martyrdom. It is desirable that attending to yourself and caring for and about others should be in balance. Once your own needs and wants are sufficiently attended to, then it is natural to want others to have what they need and want as well. In this spirit, it is appropriate and desirable to have a support team, a group of people who are committed to one another's well being and empowerment. It is a circle of friends who are dedicated to encouraging the higher self—or "the messages"—to run the show. It is a group who has learned how to discern when a friend needs to be listened to, and when that same friend needs to be gently pressed. It knows what support looks like from situation to situation, and it knows how to respond in appropriate ways.

In order to start a support group, you begin with one friend who will listen and who will be honest with you. After you have established a solid support structure between the two of you, then you may want to consider adding a third, and then a fourth, and so on. Ideally the group should not grow beyond ten, but there are exceptions. If the group consists primarily of professionals who travel a lot, then you might want to expand it so that there are always enough members available and in town to reach out to.

You don't want to get into the trap of the "I can do it alone" syndrome. This smacks of: I don't need anyone else, I can handle everything on my own. The converse of this is picking up the phone every time you feel the slightest twinge of uncertainty,

doubt, or fear. Either one is an extreme, but since binary thinking is very familiar, you may have a propensity toward one
extreme or the other. Watch out for both, since neither is what
you want.

THE
MANAGEMENT
OF CHANGE
■

In order to manage change effectively, you must understand
the dynamics of the change process. Change is extremely difficult for about 95% of the population. Most people resist
change, while others, a very small percent, thrive on it. Since
we are all creatures of habit, we tend to cling to what is familiar
to us. We unconsciously construct our frame of reference out
of all those experiences, feelings, thoughts, beliefs, attitudes,
points of view, and perceptions that we have accumulated over
the years and hold to be true. Since we hold these perceptions
as true, the frame of reference has become part of our identity.
We associate with it, and we very often think of it as ourselves.

Change disrupts and disorients our frame of reference.
When our frame of reference has become disrupted, we find
ourselves clinging to the familiar; in other words, going back
to what we know. Forging ahead into the unknown, the void,
presses us into the realms of risk-taking and of relinquishing
the familiar. Any normal human being would resist leaping
into the void, the unknown, the uncertain future.

In order to manage yourself through the change process,
you must intentionally and deliberately reinforce the direction
in which you are going and diminish the orientation you are
leaving. You must perceive the past as less attractive than
your picture of the future. You need to envision and reinforce
the vision of a positive, desirable, and inviting future. If you
let nostalgia kick in and drag you back to the memory of "the
good old days," you can forget any hopes of succeeding in your
change endeavors. Nostalgia will seduce you back to your old

frame of reference, because it is familiar, predictable, and certain. Even if your old frame of reference is undesirable, uncomfortable, painful, or traumatic, you will still gravitate to it over the new way: You associate it with your identity because of its familiarity. The transition state is so uncertain and unpredictable it is difficult to sustain without wanting to regress back to the previous state. It's like an old friend: You may not like him, but you know him so well you can't just throw him out. After all you've been through, you would have to start all over with a new one.

In any situation which involves changing from one state to another, there are three phases: the known, the transition, and the future. The present state is known, familiar, and predictable. You are less likely to want to leave any situation which is familiar. We are creatures of habit. Even if the situation is painful, you are more likely to stay with an undesirable situation rather than leave what you know.

Moving from the present, familiar state to the transition state is disruptive, and disorienting. It involves moving into the unknown, the unpredictable, the uncertain. The transition phase is highly unstable, since there is no familiarity. Most people who are unsure of their motives or reward for choosing to change, will regress in the transition state. They will retreat to what they know, not necessarily what they love, rather than aim for the future state.

The future, desired state once achieved becomes the new status quo. The future becomes the present, after you have passed through transition. Another way of saying it is, "There becomes Here when you eliminate the T." The "T" is the stage of Transition. The challenge is to manage yourself through to the desired state without letting yourself regress midway.

The following chart lists the characteristics of each phase. If you are undergoing a change, check where you are on the chart.

THE PHASES OF A "CHANGE" PROJECT

P PRESENT STATE	T TRANSITION STATE	D DESIRED STATE
■ Certain	■ Fear of loss	■ Certain
■ Predictable	■ Anxiety	■ Predictable
■ Stable	■ Alteration of F.O.R.	■ Stable
■ Defined/Familiar	■ Mini-identity crisis	■ Defined/Familiar
■ Comfortable	■ Unknown	■ Comfortable
■ Identity	■ Confused	■ Stable Identity
■ Safe	■ Active	■ Safe
■ Tangible	■ Unsettled	■ Tangible
■ Known	■ Disoriented	■ Known
■ Controllable	■ Ambiguous	■ Controllable
	■ Uncertain	■ Active
	■ Unpredictable	
	■ Foreign	
	■ Disorganized	
	■ Unstable	
	■ Risky/exciting	
	■ Uncomfortable	
	■ Dangerous	
	■ Uncontrolled	

LIVING THE PROCESS
■

There are twelve specific steps which can help you overcome negaholism. Practice living them every day of your life in order to stay happy with yourself. They are not arbitrary, but vital to the recovery process.

THE
TWELVE STEPS
TO LIVING
THE PROCESS

■

1. To enjoy every day of my life and have fun doing whatever I'm doing.
2. To feel, experience, and honor my feelings.
3. To tell the truth, my truth, to the best of my ability.
4. To look within myself for my messages, guidance, direction.
5. To focus on solutions rather than on problems.
6. To believe in myself, to believe in others, and to believe in the impossible.
7. To be committed to moving in my life; to reach out for help and/or to have a consulting session when I get off track or "stuck."
8. To love myself unconditionally, all the parts of me, and to treasure who I am.
9. To pursue my dreams, my inspiration, to follow my "Higher Self," and my messages.
10. To reach out to others, and/or to God when I need support—believing in the perfection of all and seeing my circumstances in the right perspective.
11. To be responsible for my behavior and for my own actions, and to take charge of all situations which I am able to bring to a positive resolution.
12. To regard everything in my life as a mirror, to learn a lesson, to grow, to search for the perfection in the grand scheme of things, and to self-correct lovingly.

THE
ACHIEVEMENT
OF SERENITY
■

There are nine steps to the achievement of serenity. Each step is important to the process. Ultimately the goal is to find inner peace, to end the inner battle forever. Negaholism is the absence of serenity. It is the abusive inner dialogue which keeps you from the tranquil calm of self-love.

Serenity, however, is a double-edged sword. You don't pursue serenity by giving up or being complacent, nor do you achieve it by driving compulsively. It is a balance between the polar opposites of the universe. It means not getting stuck on how you look, or how things are "supposed" to be. It doesn't mean acting in an evolved, conscious, or holy manner. It involves being genuine, real, and fully you. It involves telling the truth, and being willing to stop, feel, listen, and learn. It involves connecting with your highest self.

The "Achievement of Serenity" scale presents the various phases that a person can pass through in a lifetime if he is ultimately in search of inner peace or serenity. Any person may stop at any phase and spend the rest of his life there. Or, with reflection, introspection, and contemplation, deeper and more meaningful paths may be pursued.

By the time you reach self-actualization, you must give up your negaholic tendencies. However, you will find negaholics at every phase of the scale right on up through stardom.

SURVIVAL
The path starts with survival. Survival is the most basic phase of development, and is concerned with literally staying alive. Survival concerns have to do with food, water, shelter, and sex. If survival needs are not attended to, you die.

STRUGGLE

Struggle is the next phase beyond survival. Struggle is not so much embedded in the survival issues as it is concerned with trying to pull itself out of the quicksand of daily living. Every day is about struggling to make ends meet, and staying ahead of the treadmill which might drag you back into survival.

STABILITY

Stability reaches a plateau on which you can stand without constantly fighting off the elements and the bill collectors. When you are in stability you can take a breath, and pause for a little while on the road of life. Things have ironed out, and for the time being they are stable.

SELF-DETERMINISM

When you reach self-determinism, you have come to the conclusion that if you are going to make anything of your life it is up to you. You have now taken the bull by the horns, and you are up to the challenge of determining your own destiny.

SEEKING

When you have reached seeking, you are looking for alternative ways of doing things. You are looking for some meaning, purpose, and relevance for your life. You are searching for answers that make sense.

STRIVING

When you are at striving, you see the light at the end of the tunnel, and you want it. You keep pushing out and moving forward, eager to get there. You know you are not yet there, and you want to be, so all of your efforts are driving you forward. "Just one more" is your theme song, and you won't give up.

STARDOM

Stardom is a breakthrough. You have gotten to a rung of the ladder of "there." Your accomplishments, who you are, or some special aspect of you receives public acclaim. There are rewards, often monetary, and recognition, so that you may experience being "there." If you have no spiritual orientation, then "stardom" is "there" for you; if you do, then you know there is more.

SELF-ACTUALIZATION

Beyond stardom, the self-actualized person knows that wealth and fame, although desirable, do not make you happy. The self-actualized person is aligned in words and actions. The self-actualized person "walks his talk," and has the ability to manifest his wants at will. The self-actualized person is an expert at that which he has chosen to be his life's work, work that is the vehicle he uses to master the art of living.

SERENITY

Serenity is the state of calmness; peace; brightness; clarity; certainty. It is the place of natural knowingness. It is the "I can" self transcended to the state of "I know." It is a state that is centered and knowing. It means living in your "I can" self, knowing who you are, what you want, and how to get it.

Any negaholic can achieve the state of serenity. You will go through each stage. You can embark on the road to recovery, and completely conquer your negaholism. You need the desire, the willingness, and the commitment. You can do it. Believe in yourself, trust that you can, take one day at a time, and ask God for help. You too can have everything that you've dreamed. *Love yourself, trust your choices, and everything is possible.*

APPENDICES

■

RESOURCES

■

This book presents many different techniques and tools which you can use with yourself to manage your daily life. The one strong recommendation that I would give to someone who wants to take charge of his compulsive behavior and start the process of recovery is to reach out for help, support, and encouragement. It is difficult to break old patterns and change behaviors by yourself. There are some people who can do it, but the vast majority need the reinforcement and follow-up that only others can provide. Outside help also keeps us honest with ourselves.

There are many different kinds of help and support. Friends and family are one really good source, provided that they have no personal agenda and have your best interests at heart.

Professional help is also enormously beneficial. You can use a personal consultant, a counselor, a therapist, a social worker, a minister, or a psychiatrist. It is up to you to determine which you prefer, depending on approach, financial considerations, and scheduling.

There are several agencies that concentrate on dependent, compulsive behaviors. They are specialists in their fields. If you have compulsive behavior which is manifested in any of these forms, the following list may be useful.

ALCOHOLICS ANONYMOUS,
    468 Park Avenue South, New York, N.Y. 10016
    (212) 686–1100
COCAINE ANONYMOUS,
    6125 Washington Avenue, Suite 202, Culver City, Ca.
    90232 (213) 839–1141
NARCOTICS ANONYMOUS, World Service Office,
    16155 Wyandotte Street, Van Nuys, Ca. 91406,
    (818) 780–3951
AMERICAN CANCER SOCIETY,
    4 West 35th Street, New York, N.Y. 10001 (212) 736–3030
NATIONAL ANOREXIC AID SOCIETY,
    P.O. Box 29461, Columbus, Ohio 43229 (614) 436–1112
OVEREATERS ANONYMOUS,
    P.O. Box 92870, Los Angeles, Ca. 90009 (213) 320–7941
GAMBLERS ANONYMOUS, National Service Office,
    P.O. Box 17173, Los Angeles, Ca. 90017 (213) 386–8789
THE AMERICAN SOCIETY OF SEX EDUCATORS, COUN-
SELORS AND THERAPISTS,
    11 Dupont Circle, NW, Suite 220, Washington, DC
    20036–1207 (202) 462–1171

THE
TWELVE
STEPS
■

Since I mentioned the Alcoholics Anonymous motto, "One day at a time," I thought it would be helpful to include their twelve steps here. Over the years, these twelve steps have been enormously instrumental in the recovery process for alcoholics. They are a useful reference when battling compulsive behavior patterns, specifically those that are alcohol related. I have many clients who find solace in reading through and working the steps. Use them if and when you feel the desire in your own recovery process.

THE TWELVE STEPS

1. We admitted we were powerless over alcohol—that our lives had become unmanageable.
2. Came to believe that a power greater than ourselves could restore us to sanity.
3. Made a decision to turn our will and our lives over to the care of God as we understood him.
4. Made a searching and fearless moral inventory of ourselves.
5. Admitted to God, to ourselves, and to another human being the exact nature of our wrongs.
6. Were entirely ready to have God remove all these defects of character.
7. Humbly asked him to remove our shortcomings.
8. Made a list of all persons we had harmed, and became willing to make amends to them all.
9. Made direct amends to such people wherever possible, except when to do so would injure them or others.
10. Continued to take personal inventory, and when we were wrong, promptly admitted it.
11. Sought through prayer and meditation to improve our conscious contact with God as we understood him, praying only for knowledge of his will for us and the power to carry that out.
12. Having had a spiritual awakening as the result of these steps, we tried to carry this message to alcoholics, and to practice these principles in all our affairs.

The Twelve Steps are reprinted with permission of Alcoholics Anonymous World Services, Inc.

SUGGESTED
READING
LIST
■

The Art of Selfishness by David Seabury. New York: Pocket Books, 1937.

Changing Lives Through Redecision Therapy by Mary McClure Goulding and Robert Goulding. New York: Grove Press, 1979.

Children of Alcoholism: A Survivors' Manual by Judith Seixas and Geraldine Youcha. New York: Crown Publishers, 1985.

Don't Say Yes When You Want to Say No by Herbert Fensterheim and Jean Baer. New York: Dell Publishing, 1975.

The Intuitive Edge by Philip Goldberg. New York: Jeremy P. Tarcher, Inc., 1983.

The Magic of Thinking Big by David J. Schwartz. New York: Prentice Hall, 1965.

Self-Esteem by Matthew McKay and Patrick Fanning. Oakland, California: New Harbinger Press, 1987.

Skills for Success by Adele Scheele. New York: Random House, 1979.

Vital Lies, Simple Truths by Daniel Goleman. New York: Simon & Schuster, 1985.

When Society Becomes an Addict by Anne Wilson Schaef. New York: Harper & Row, 1987.

Winning Life's Toughest Battles by Julius Segal. New York: Ballantine Books, 1986.

BIBLIOGRAPHY

Bradshaw, J. *John Bradshaw on The Family: A Revolutionary Way of Self-Discovery.* Pompano Beach, Florida: Health Communications, Inc., 1988.

Branden, N. *The Psychology of Self-Esteem.* New York: Bantam Books, 1971.

———. *The Disowned Self.* New York: Bantam Books, 1973.

———. *Honoring the Self: The Psychology of Confidence and Respect.* New York: Bantam Books, 1985.

Carson, Richard D. *Taming Your Gremlin: A Guide to Enjoying Yourself.* New York and San Francisco: Harper & Row, 1986.

Clarke, J. I. *Self-Esteem: A Family Affair.* Minnesota: Winston Press, 1978.

Cloninger, Robert C.; Reich, Theodore; Siguardson, Soren; Knorring, Anne-Liis; and Bonman, Michael. "Effects of Change in Alcohol Use Between Generations on Inheritance of Alcohol Abuse." In *Alcoholism: Origins and Outcome,* edited by R. M. Rose and J. Barrett. New York: Raven Press, 1988.

Einstein, S., ed. *The International Journal of the Addictions* (1987): 22:1167–1324.

Fillmore, Kaye Middleton. "Alcohol Problems from a Sociological Perspective." In *Alcoholism: Origins and Outcome,* edited by R. M. Rose and J. Barrett. New York: Raven Press, 1988.

Fingarette, H. *Heavy Drinking: The Myth of Alcoholism as a Disease.* University of California Press, 1988.

Forward, S., and J. Torres. *Men Who Hate Women and the Women Who Love Them.* New York: Bantam Books, 1986.

Goodwin, Donald W. *Is Alcoholism Hereditary?* New York: Ballantine Books, 1986.

Gravitz, Herbert L., and Julie D. Bowden. *Recovery: A Guide for Adult Children of Alcoholics.* New York: Simon & Schuster, 1987.

Guze, Samuel B.; Cloninger, Robert C.; Martin, Ronald; and Clayton, Paula J. "Alcoholism as a Medical Disorder." In *Alcoholism: Origins and Outcome,* edited by R. M. Ross and J. Barrett. New York: Raven Press, 1988.

Helzer, John E., Canino, Glorisa J.; Hwu, Hai-Gwo; Bland, Roger C.; and Yeh, Eng-Kung. "A Cross-National Comparison of Population Surveys with the Diagnostic Interview Schedule." In *Alcoholism: Origins and Outcome,* edited by R. M. Rose and J. Barrett. New York: Raven Press, 1988.

Jensen, M. "Understanding Addictive Behavior and the Theory of

Psychological Reversals." *American Journal of Health Promotion* (Winter 1987): 48:57.

Kagan, D., and R. Squires. "Addictive Aspects of Physical Exercise." *Journal of Sports Medicine* (1985): 25: 227–237.

McKay, M., and P. Fanning. *Self-Esteem.* Oakland, California: New Harbinger Press, 1987.

Meyer, Roger E. "Overview of the Concept of Alcoholism." In *Alcoholism: Origins and Outcome,* edited by R. M. Rose and J. Barrett. New York: Raven Press, 1988.

Milkman, H., and H. J. Shaffer. *The Addictions: Multidisciplinary Perspectives and Treatments.* Lexington, Massachussetts: Lexington Books, 1987.

———, and S. Sunderwirth. *Craving for Ecstasy: The Consciousness and Chemistry of Escape.* Lexington, Massachussetts: Lexington Books, 1987.

Miller, W. "Brief Report: Addictive Behavior and the Theory of Psychological Reversals." *Addictive Behaviors* (1985): 10: 177–80.

Murray, Robert M.; Gurling, Hugh; Bernadt, Morris W.; and Clifford, Christine A. "Economics, Occupation, and Genes: A British Perspective." In *Alcoholism: Origins and Outcome,* edited by R. M. Rose and J. Barrett. New York: Raven Press, 1988.

Norwood, R. *Women Who Love Too Much: When You Keep Wishing and Hoping He'll Change.* Los Angeles, California: Jeremy P. Tarcher, 1988.

Peck, M. S. *The Road Less Traveled.* New York: Touchstone Books (A Simon & Schuster Imprint), 1978.

Peele, S. *Visions of Addiction: Major Contemporary Perspectives on Addiction and Alcoholism.* Lexington, Massachusetts: Lexington Books, 1988.

———. "What I Would Most Like to Know: How Can Addiction Occur with Other Than Drug Involvements?" *British Journal of Addiction* (1985): 80:23–25.

Restak, Richard. *The Brain: The Last Frontier.* New York: Warner Books, 1987.

Robins, Lee N.; Helzer, John E.; Przybeck, Thomas R.; and Regier, Darrell A. "Alcohol Disorders in the Community: A Report from the Epidemiological Catchment Area." In *Alcoholism: Origins and Outcome,* edited by R. M. Rose and J. Barrett. New York: Raven Press, 1988.

Schaef, A. W. *When Society Becomes an Addict.* New York and San Francisco: Harper & Row, 1987.

Vaillant, George E. "Some Differential Effects of Genes and Environment on Alcoholism." In *Alcoholism: Origins and Outcome,* edited by R. M. Rose and J. Barrett, New York: Raven Press, 1988.

Witkin, G. *Quick Fixes & Small Comforts: How Every Woman Can Resist Those Irresistible Urges.* New York: Villard Books, 1988.

Woititz, Janet G. *Adult Children of Alcoholics.* Pompano Beach, Florida: Health Communications, Inc., 1983.

If you are interested in being on a negaholic mailing list so that you are informed about lectures, presentations, seminars, workshops, or trainings in your area, please write or call:

NEGAHOLICS
P.O. Box 824
Pacific Palisades, CA. 90272

(800) 321-NEGA

PLEASE NOTE: Negaholics is not a part of Alcoholics Anonymous or any Twelve Step Program. Negaholics is, however, in active support of all the Twelve Step Programs.

ABOUT THE AUTHOR

CHÉRIE CARTER-SCOTT is an entrepreneur, lecturer, and seminar leader; she is chairman of the board and president of Motivation Management Service, Inc., a firm specializing in personal growth and professional training programs. She is also president of MMS Institute (Corporate Services) whose management consultants custom-design programs for corporations. Her corporate clients have included IBM, GTEL, AMI, Burger King, American Express, and *Better Homes and Gardens*. She is a Ph.D. candidate at the Fielding Institute in Santa Barbara, and lives in Los Angeles, California, with her family.